To every person who ever
told me to smile when
I didn't feel like it

ANGRY BLACK GIRL

[ELEXUS JIONDE]

CONTENTS

INTELEXUAL MEDIA

The Angry Black Girl

I have been a lot of black girls in my twenty-three years of life. There are the early phases of myself that I look back on with amusement and disbelief, where my identity was shaped by the stuffy environment of a surreptitiously segregated elementary school. I was a good girl, adorned with braided hair and beads. I was a pious black girl, complete with prayers and bible verse themed mumbles. I was even a token black girl among a circle of upper-middle-class white people. Then there was middle and high school, both breeding grounds for confusion and experimentation. I was definitely a fast black girl, whose sprouting body caused as much attention as it did judgment. I was a suicidal black girl, who reacted to sexual assault with razor blades to the forearm for both attention and catharsis. I was a weird alternative black girl who wore giant Hot Topic hair bows, listened to Panic! At The Disco, and even fitted vampire fangs to her teeth for everyday wear. At the same time, I was a ratchet black girl who got a tongue ring for her 18th birthday, twerked, and talked explicitly and loudly whenever she felt the whim. But there was also a smart and dedicated black girl, who flipped between colloquialisms and million dollar words like the pages of a book.

But more often than not, I have been an angry black girl. Throughout my life, even when I wasn't angry, I was often told that I sounded or looked like it by people who didn't want to listen to what I had to say. Even when I softened my words or thought I looked pleasant, someone was telling me to calm down. This was often at my customer service jobs. Apparently, it's my face, which when not stimulated by conversation or orgasm, sits naturally in a placid state. Even after a genuine smile, my face snaps back into what is annoyingly called "resting bitch mode".

Last Fall, while working in an upscale upper east side fitness club where fresh towels are soaked in eucalyptus and kept chilled in refrigerators, I had no idea my face disgruntled so many customers. I'd be happy and pumped from Starbucks cold brew, though a bit anxious to get through an eight-hour opening shift. After three years out of customer service work, I guess you could say I was a little rusty. But I was nice to club members, learning their names and indulging in the most asinine of conversations with them. When Housewife A lost her easily replaceable Black Amex card, I provided a sympathetic ear while wondering if I could afford an eye exam and a new pair of glasses. When Housewife B complained that her husband surprised her with a vacation to St. Tropez instead of St. Barts, I reverberated her outrage while inwardly speculating how many taxes were being taken out of my next $900 paycheck.

In the four months that I worked at that luxury gym, I shat out forty hours of labor a week, which I hadn't done since high school. Forty hours of fake smiling. Forty hours of inwardly digging for real empathy to serve my daily human reminders of income disparity. Forty hours of drained energy that destroyed my enthusiasm to work on my own projects at home. Forty hours of standing on my feet for $11 per hour. When my first employee evaluation came, I was disappointed to see that clients said I looked mean. I had been nice, but evidently, my face betrayed me. I told a co-worker. He, a black Dominican who said Trump might save the country, replied that all black girls look mean.

The mean black girl stereotype is often looped in with the dumb ghetto girl trope, so it's no surprise that my appearance has encouraged negative thoughts about my intellectual abilities. At the same upscale fitness club, there was a personal trainer who gave me the creeps, in addition to routinely pissing me off. He disrespected my personal space, joked about sex despite my obvious discomfort, and regularly talked about my breast size. He also fancied himself an authority on politics and social issues, so once or twice a week he'd come to the main desk and deliver an unwanted lecture that I'd nod impatiently to, willing myself not to argue so that he'd leave sooner. After all, it was a new workplace and I didn't want to start any beef early because of my opinions. Not that he ever actually asked for them, because he didn't care to know them. Eventually, after one titty joke too far, I blew up on him and started acting extra cold   9 towards him. He got the hint and kept his distance. But in October, he stumbled across my infamous 9/11 twitter thread. He came to me amazed. "Wow, I had no idea you were smart! Like, no offense, I just thought you were this hood girl," he exclaimed, glancing at my 1.5-inch acrylics and severely raised eyebrow. My face must have said it all, as he began to backtrack. "That's not a bad thing! I didn't mean- you're smart! Just take the compliment. You're always so angry, Lexi! Just smile," he laughed, trying to play off the last few seconds as some big joke that I was about to overreact to. As I carefully decided how to respond, a member approached the desk. I forced a smile, like I had been doing much more frequently after my evaluation, and checked her in. When I turned back to the personal trainer, the smile was gone. But I did not say what I wanted to say because then there would be another employee break room rumor floating around about the black girl at the front desk with the bad attitude. The spit in my mouth turned to acid in the split second that he looked at me for a response to his 'compliment'. I found compromise between an expletive-laced rebuke and gratitude for his shady comment. "Preciate it," I mumbled.

I've spent my life trying to avoid being labeled the angry black girl. Up through my youth and into my young adult years, I've never had a problem expressing my opinions on things like pop culture (and later sex), but when it came to discussing the nuances of racism and sexism, I tried to tiptoe around controversy. A lot of the time, that has meant keeping my mouth shut when something offends or concerns me... and usually for the sake of keeping a job. It's hard to imagine that time not too long ago when being conscious of black and gender issues was considered annoying, counterproductive, and bitter. After all, as my 10th grade civics teacher told me, "Racism is over. America is for everybody." But that's a damned lie. Like most of my peers, I was socialized into accepting America's subtle racial hierarchy and was never expected to challenge it. But as a black woman, I was also socialized to not challenge sexism or misogyny.

Responding to backhanded compliments and microaggressions with honesty is how black women get alienated and maligned. As a black woman, I am the complete opposite of the white man, who is allowed to express anger or discomfort without being labeled bitter by broader society because of his gender and race. White women can voice discontent because they are white. They will still appear feminine and worthy of protection and love, especially when they fulfill ideal beauty standards. Black men can be angry because they're men- and sexism dictates that men are logical. But for me? The human at a racial and sexual disadvantage? I am bitter and illogical. I am not worth listening to. My musings on racism are bitter to white folks and my thoughts on toxic masculinity are bitter to black men. At a deeper intersection, my economic status as a poor black woman makes my criticisms of capitalism bitter and illogical too. At every turn, someone is trying to tell me what I am instead of listening to what I am actually saying. At all times, I (and many other black women who wish to be heard) must be careful to not come across as angry or bitter- a spectacular feat when we have been stereotyped as those two things for nearly two centuries. Angry black women get ignored or ridiculed, even if they have a right to be angry.

I want you to know that the initial title for this collection of essays was *Angry Black Bitch*. It is a phrase   11 that has been hurled at me a lot since I first went viral in September of 2016, usually in response to my tweet threads that challenged popular conceptions about race in America. I wanted to use *Angry Black Bitch* as a tongue in cheek retort to my critics. While the name felt perfect at first, eventually I became worried that it was too offensive, despite my sound reasoning for using it. I worried that the title would immediately put people off from what I had to say. Even though this is a collection of angry essays on race, religion, and gender, I was wary of scaring away potential readers. But why? After all, *Angry Black Girl* isn't a subtle title. Years from now when I'm building a charter school or being lampooned by the press for hurting a deserving white woman's feelings, *Angry Black Girl* will probably be used as a weapon against me. I could have just kept the title as *Angry Black Bitch*, scaring off easily appalled readers, but a small part of me still yearns to be heard by people who don't want to hear me.

Even as my rage at injustice continues to pump through my veins, an even smaller part of me still wants to avoid being called the angry black bitch. Though admittedly that part of me, the girl who wants to be the smiling black employee who makes rich white clients let her keep her job, is slowly dying. She is on her way to being a distant memory like many girls I have been in my life. Some girls, like the ratchet and smart versions of Lexi, are here to stay. Other manifestations of my identity have died slow deaths. The pious girl who couldn't fathom rejecting religion. The good little girl with the beads and braids who didn't cuss because she thought her mother could hear her. The girl who wanted to be the "cool black" to her white buddies. The girl with the obnoxiously large sequined bow in her chemically damaged hair, all of her accessories adorned with Hello Kitty. The sad girl who wanted to die because she felt her life had no purpose. These girls came and went, but one has lingered. She is the girl who wants to avoid being called angry and bitter, by white people but especially by black men. For years she has tempered herself and underreacted to racial and sexist jabs, thinking that voicing her disgust or anger would just further the stereotype and hold her back.

So I made one last compromise for that sensitive and dying girl still lurking inside of me, omitting the word bitch from the title of this book. It is the last time I will allow her to dictate what I say and how. Towering over the little girl who doesn't want to be called angry is a grown woman who doesn't care if you like what she has to say. It is her voice that speaks to you from these pages, her rage that calls out for your contemplation. It's been a long time coming, but she's here to stay.

The Evil Stepmother

I don't recall my exact age when I became aware of the fact that I hated my father. It was a slow process that percolated for years from a medley of events that still remain fresh in my mind. My mom says I was 10 or 11 when I came to her and told her I never wanted to go back to his house again and that I hated him, but I still went until I was about 13. To be clear, my mother never badmouthed my father around me. She, like many moms, didn't influence my opinion. All of the opinions I have of my father were assembled from my own interactions (or lack thereof) with him. There is an abundance of reasons why I hate him, but the most important one is how he allowed someone named Angela to damage me. But first, let me give you some background info.

Cedric Donnell White was about to eat a hot sauce covered pork chop when he instructed a friend to bring Tammy Peake over to the table so he could do the 1991 version of shooting his shot. He had somehow spied her above the fray of flattops and braided up-dos, decked out in cutoff denim shorts, a black vest a la Janet Jackson, a white t-shirt, and black sandals. The scene was the cafeteria at Barber-Scotia college. It was the first day, and my mother had shooed my nana and papa away with finesse after settling into her dorm room. My mother saw Cedric and thought he was cute so she agreed to meet him. She slowly made her way through the crowd of future thrift store clothing clad freshmen to the handsome nigga smiling broadly at her from across the cafeteria. "Hello," Tamara said politely when she finally arrived at his table. He took one long look at her and drank in her thick figure like it was cold milk, as if he was carefully choosing his first words to speak to her. "If you play your cards right this could be you," he said. He took a savage bite out of his pork chop. Hot sauce dribbled down his chin.

Though my mother didn't initially give into the charming, attractive, and clearly horny "Scooter" (as he had been called since childhood), they began dating later that school year. For a while, the relationship was good, as Scooter was funny and charismatic. They shared a love for Tupac and roasting people with jokes. Before long, however, my father was sleeping with other women, habitually lying, and regularly getting fired from the low-level jobs he managed to get. But still, my mother hung on. She thought that she could change him. He was a DIY project in the making, she just had to hurdle over his bullshit and hold him down. It's no surprise   15 that by the spring of 1993 she found out that she was pregnant. My mom wasn't initially excited, and to this day I'm still not sure if she's joking when she says she missed her "Wednesday appointment". But reluctance turned to enthusiasm, and by the third month, she was latching classical music blasting Walkman headphones onto her belly so that I could be stimulated in the womb. It was a trick she saw on *The Montell Williams Show*. My father teased her and said it was stupid, but Tamara kept on playing her classical music cassettes for little Lexi. She even kept a diary, in which she wrote sporadic entries addressed to me. She noted her obsession with Chinese food, which as anyone who knows me will tell you, is one of my favorite things. Tamara also documented the arguments and lows of her relationship with my father.

She soon visited his hometown of Statesville, a tiny country town about forty-five minutes from Charlotte. His family immediately hated my mother, who was considered both sadity and city. The hatred was so thick that it reverberated years later whenever I visited as a child, and I remember family members being inexplicably mean until I got older. To make matters more complicated, my father had a newborn daughter and another one on the way (whose paternity was alleged to be up in the air between Scooter and his cousin) with a white woman named Lora. Away from the predominately black atmosphere of Barber Scotia, my mom noticed something. She attended parties where grinning white women called out to Scooter and openly lusted after him. His friends looked were suprised that my mother wasn't white. His other exes were white. My mother asked him plainly, "Why the fuck do you fuck with so many white women?" His answer? "Because they do whatever I say."

My mother was turned off by this and soon broke up with him, preparing to take care of me without his assistance. When she gave birth to me in January of 1994, she was living at home with my nana and papa. It would only be a few months before she was tired of living with her parents, but on a limited budget, her options were tight. So she scraped together some savings and recruited Scooter to move with us into a hood-luxe townhome on Bradford Drive in Charlotte before settling a few months later into a complex called Roseland. It wasn't long before Scooter was reneging on his promise to pay half of the bills. While my mother busted her ass as a Pre-K teacher to care for the household and to keep my little mind stimulated, my father lost money, lost jobs, and lost his damned mind.

My mother recalled a time when my father got a job at the Adams Mark Hotel and two weeks later fucked a co-worker in one of the rooms. Scooter then went around bragging about the tryst to his male work buds, and all the men began harassing the woman. They'd make little sex jokes whenever the female co-worker walked by, my father at the center of the immature comments that torpedoed her as a hoe. Eventually, it became too much for her. She went to human resources and he was fired. He promptly went home and told my mother that he had been laid off. It was months later when my mother learned the truth.

Even though Tamara hated Scooter's constant lying, cheating, and periods of unemployment, there was one thing she adored. He was a very attentive father to me and made it a point to play with me and inter- 17 act with me as much as possible. Despite this quality, Scooter was still a dog. By the time I was three years old my mother had grown disgusted by him. One day she woke up next to him in bed and realized he wouldn't be a good figure in my life and that he would never make her happy in a relationship. He had to go. She waited for him to wake up and shared the news. "When it was over for us, it was like yall broke up too," my mother told me as I wrote down notes for this essay. When he moved out two days after the breakup, he was homeless before briefly rooming with a few other men in Charlotte.

A few weeks later he had a new girlfriend, a white woman named Angela. She was a large woman with a pretty face. Sweet, docile, and a mother of one chubby faced daughter named Larissa, my father thought he had hit the jackpot. She had a fulltime job and an apartment, two things my father just couldn't resist. In addition to the fact that Angela's baby father consistently paid child support, the paternal grandparents were financially supportive. My father wouldn't need to do much to take care of Angela- but he could get taken care of.

Unbeknownst to me, at the time a child unaware of race politics and identities, Angela was the first white latina I ever encountered. She spoke French and Spanish fluently, having picked up the latter from her Cuban father. I met this smiling woman at the age of 5. "Oh, Cedric! She's so cute!" she gushed, wrapping me in a hug. I met her daughter, a brown and quiet three-year-old with curly hair. Angela seemed nice, and she was a welcome change from my father's male roommates. As a five- year-old I really didn't see anything wrong with her being with my father. A few months later, they were married. Years later my mother would tell me that my father called her the night before his wedding, terrified that he was making a mistake in marrying Angela. But whatever terror he felt did not stop him from walking down the aisle and into a future of financial security with a woman who, in his words, would do whatever he said. On that snowy winter day, my father entered both he and I into Angela's unforeseen torment. As soon as the wedding was over, Angela hatched into the true version of herself: demanding, condescending, and insanely hateful of both me and my mother. I could write a book about all of the things my stepmother ever did to me, but for brevity, let me give you a rundown.

Angela became pregnant immediately. My father was in a constant state of unemployment, and every weekend that I'd get dropped off at their apartment, my mother would pull him aside about child support. The jealousy bubbled inside of Angela, but her fear of my mom meant she kept her mouth shut. I'd shuffle inside to the apartment to see her peeking through the curtains at my parents, her face etched with anger and melodrama. She'd shoot me a glare, but say nothing as I went to go play with Larissa. Like clockwork, the arguing would begin when my father would come through the door a few minutes after. "Are you still fucking her, Cedric?" she would bellow. Doors would slam. Scooter would yell. Angela would cry. Then it would get real quiet and dinner would be served. Angela would act like nothing happened. My father would sit at the table with his jaw clenched and his temple throbbing. One of these nights got so bad that Angela got bold with my mother over the phone and ended up getting her ass beat. I distinctly remember a potted plant smashing. The police were called. These episodes surrounding the possibility of my mother being her husband's mistress eventually stopped when Angela found out the subject of her jealousy was in a lesbian relationship.

She shifted gears. Though already a Catholic, she became more religious. I remember her forcefully trying to get me to understand that "God created Adam and Eve, not Steve." A few times during bedtime prayer she took special care to pray for my mothers heathen soul. But Angela's resentment for my mother manifested itself in other ways. For starters, she commented frequently on the poor quality of my hair whenever she was doing Larissa's. She loved to remind me that she was a graduate of UNC-Chapel Hill, and she'd ask slyly, "Your mom dropped out of college, didn't she?" My stepmother also told me I wasn't allowed to call my dad "dad", saying that it wasn't fair to her daughter. She insisted I call him "Papi" instead. Once while pregnant Angela explained to me, a child, that I was a bastard because my mother and father weren't married when they had me. She laughed, pawing at a bowl of red grapes balanced on her enormous belly before calling me a bastard as if it was the funniest thing in the world. She rarely said things like this in front of my father, instead opting to reserve her contempt towards me for when he was out working or cheating on her.

In one of those grand times my father was missing in action, my tooth came out while I was in time-out. I was eight or nine. Blood gushed from my gum, soaking my chin and shirt. When I got up from time-out to show Angela, she had no sympathy. She returned me to the time-out chair to sit with my bleeding mouth, telling me that she would have "papi" beat me if I got any blood on her carpet. I sat in agony for the next hour, swallowing my own blood until a smiling Angela told me I could go rinse my mouth out.

In 2003 when my father and Angela moved into a tri-level home in South Charlotte, their marriage got even worse. Angela made sure to mark the basement as my room, where it was the coldest place in the house and there was a roach infestation. The windows were caked with dust and were terrifying at night when the shadows from outside trees danced against them. When I complained, my dad did nothing and Angela chucked me a night light. To spite her, I began sleeping on the living room couch and finally on the floor at the foot of her daughter's bed. Once on vacation Angela got upset with me for something my father did and refused to feed me for the remainder of the trip, deliberately making meals for her children and leaving me to stare hungrily while my father probably cheated on her in a strip club, too far away for me to tell him what she had done until he came back hours later sweaty and high from weed.

You may be wondering where my father was during these events. I learned early on that my father was not my ally. His strategy often including bribing me with forehead kisses into apologizing to Angela for whatever she was upset about. This could be anything from me saying "my dad", fixing myself a sandwich, or watching a PG-13 movie without her permission. She loved to get angry at little things such as these, infractions of rules she placed for her own daughter who was a whole two years younger than me. When I could, I'd get permission from Scooter on something like watching *Family Guy,* and Angela, who wasn't even my biological parent, would get angry at him for allegedly undermining her authority. So Scooter preferred not to deal with it. "It" including her jabs at my hair, mother, and bastard   21 status.

For most of her emotional abuse, Scooter was at work, looking for work, or laying in some woman's bed trying to convince her to give him some money. Every transgression he committed against her I felt later. Whenever I told my mom, she would show up to beat Angela's ass, and once she actually got to do it. But after Angela pulled me aside when I was 10 or 11 and told me that she would get my mom thrown in jail if I didn't stop "telling lies on her", I stopped giving a fuck. I remembered how scared I was that my mother would get arrested. So I said nothing. I'd go to my dad's house with an awful attitude, spending most of my time ignoring Angela or challenging her authority.

Angela was an atrocious woman, but her hostilities and micro-aggressions did not disgust me as much as my father's actions. I had loved that man. He looked like Tupac, watched Wizard of Oz with me, and always had a stack of yellow Wendy's napkins in the glove compartment of his gray Nissan. He called me "Lexus" or "sweetheart" in that smooth country drawl of his. He taught me the rules of "Punch Baggy! Volkswagen!" Its been so long since I interacted with him that I don't even recall what our conversations used to be about, but I fucked with him. So when he stood by and let Angela torment me, or didn't react when I told him what she was doing, the love I had for him rotted into resentment and hatred.

Everything about him, from his clothing choices to the Newports he smoked disgusted me. I recoiled from his hugs or forehead kisses and dreaded going over to his house where he would ask me about my life and make me uncomfortable. He was not the man I used to know. By the age of thirteen, I was done visiting my father. I wasn't around for his subsequent divorce from Angela.

In the years since my childhood, bits of "you're grown now" information about my fathers past made his relationship with Angela (and mine) more painfully clear. My dad is one of those black men who believes white women are superior to black ones. As he informed my mother, they've got less attitude and "know how to treat a man". The latter was an especially important trait to my father, as he regularly got fired from jobs and needed someone secure to fall back on. While Angela mistreated his daughter, he mooched off her CMS teaching salary, opened credit cards with her good credit, and impregnated her a second time. Every time I'd confront him about Angela being cruel, he'd make an excuse for her that usually ended with me apologizing or begging for a reconciliation just so she would stop giving him the silent treatment.

I originally thought that Angela hated me because of my mother, but as I got older it became deeper than that. She never showed the same level of contempt to my older half-siblings, who were mixed like her kids. In her mind, I was a poor extension of my father's genes. Angela herself was not all evil. She was very smart and was always dropping interesting trivia. She tried teaching me Spanish, she made amazing empanadas, and her good credit netted a family trip to a timeshare in Miami. It was my first and only childhood trip to a major beach that wasn't Myrtle Beach. So shout out to her for that. But she wasn't a good person. She was a white identifying Latina who loved black dick and felt superior to black women.

From her comments about my hair, to her adoption of black culture (she said nigga and adored rap music), to her utter disrespect of the child of a man she claimed to love, it is clear to me as an adult that Angela was a major influence on my early thoughts on interracial romance and myself. For years I grappled with irrational hatred of white women who dated black men. I questioned my value as a black girl in the shadow of her microaggressions. Angela set the framework for a lot of my interactions with white women. Her pattern, though unrecognizable to me as a youth, was simplistic and genius. Torment me. Wait for me to react. Play the victim role to my father. Relish in the apology (and playing the bigger person role) by offering forgiveness that was never needed. Repeat. This is where my hatred for my father lies. More than his unwillingness to pay child support, more than his views on white women as life partners, and more than his treatment of my mother, I hate him for allowing a white woman to make his daughter feel inferior. The first black man I ever was supposed to rely on let me down.

To this day I meet people from Charlotte who had a Spanish or French class with Mrs. White at North Mecklenburg High School. Apparently, she was a really dope and funny teacher to classrooms of predominantly black students. To them, it is unfathomable that Mrs. White was emotionally abusive and neglectful to her black step-daughter, and they tell me so.

Racist White Women
[An American Legacy]

My freshman year of college my 5'1 blonde roommate
Elizabeth busted into our suite and called me a "fucking
bitch" over something I said on Twitter. She was drunk
and aggressive. I was sober and half-sleep. I told her
to go away and she advanced into my personal space,
yelling and knocking over my perfume bottles. I looked
at her in disbelief. Just last week we had shared a heart
to heart over Russian vodka on the floor of our closet,
discussing her old heroin addiction and my traumatic
early high school years. She gritted her teeth and told
me she'd kick my ass, then left. In the next hour, I got
into a screaming match with some white guys from
down the hall who came out of the room to protect her
when I came looking for her; and I ended up sleeping in
the basement. The next week I was served a restrain-

25

ing order and told I was facing expulsion from school-plus I was forced to move out immediately. To sweeten the shit stew, little Elizabeth told the school that I was a drug addict and I was subsequently forced to take drug tests and $100 drug counseling sessions for two semesters. Though Elizabeth had threatened me first, she had no issue convincing the school that the 5'7 black girl was a danger to her personal safety. It wasn't the first or last time a white woman would use her privilege to slight me, but I thought about this particular incident recently when watching the wildly popular Jordan Peele creation *Get Out*.

While the male members of the Armitage family were aggressive and at times openly hostile before the films big climax, Rose and her mother Missy were sickeningly sweet. As I watched the plot unfold on screen, I, wondered if Rose was in on her parents' nefarious plot to hypnotize Chris. As soon as Rose said "nobody messes with my man" (forgive me if this isn't verbatim, I saw the film on a very hazy weekend in New Orleans and I consider myself fortunate to remember the basics of the plot) in the car on the way to her parents, I knew the bitch wasn't to be trusted. The way she said *my man* inexplicably annoyed me and I instantly disliked her. But then my guilt kicked in. **Not all white women suck**, I reasoned with myself. Maybe it was my silly prejudices. Maybe she's not a villain. Maybe she's just some white girl who might get caught up in some shit. With those considerations in mind, I plunged my hand into my bucket of buttered popcorn and waited to find out. After Missy pulled her little teacup trick on Chris to help him kick his nicotine addiction, I tried to not let my mind go into bitter black woman mode. **Not all white women suck.** I decided that Rose had been hypnotized by her mother into participating in the dark Armitage family secret. My theory felt more plausible after Rose and Chris had a teary heart to heart while white people bid for the privilege of owning him. But later, as Chris flipped through the damning photos from the closet, I knew what my gut instinct had told me to be true. Rose, like a lot of white women, sucked.

Rose and Missy showed concern, had manners, and kept their tempers in check while their male counterparts reeked of irrationality, violence, and oddity. But by the end of the film their masks of delicate white femininity were peeled back to reveal hateful monsters. As a historian, this spoke to me on a spiritual level. America's past is rife with kind-faced white women who exploited, abused, or accused black people for their own benefit. Because white supremacy is rooted in patriarchy, it's often too easy to overlook white women under the notion that they too are oppressed. But it is prudent to remember that though oppressed, the status of white women has been and continues to be higher than both black men and women. Even if considered the white man's inferior, they are still the white man's counterpart. After all, 20th-century racism was heavily fueled by the white man's destructive desire to keep their women safe from black rapists. This has led to an odd status for white women in American society.

Because they have traditionally been symbols of femininity, they lack not only hostile reputations of hatred and violence given to white and black men but also the angry trope bestowed upon black women. This privilege has allowed white women and their special brand of racism to exist, virtually unchecked, in a variety of forms over the centuries.

The Slave Holder's Counterpart

Take 19th-century slaveholder wife Mary Epps. As detailed by Solomon Northup in *12 Years a Slave*, Mary Epps became jealous of her husband Edwin's frequent rapes of a slave girl named Patsey. Mary began beating Patsey, taking no womanly sympathy for her brutal sexual assaults, instead reducing her to a black jezebel interested in sleeping with her husband. Mary encouraged her husband to discipline Patsey after she left the plantation without permission, leading him to crack his whip at her over 50 times. Slavery is checkered with untold numbers of Patseys, who were dual victims of both their male and female masters. "One white lady that lived near us at McBean slipped in a colored gals room and cut her baby's head clean off cause it belonged to her husband." recalled a former slave being interviewed in the *WPA Slave Narrative Project.*

White Feminists AKA Frenemies

Historically, when white feminists have cried out about the injustices of sexism, they often ignored racism- or perpetuated it. As famed suffragist Elizabeth Cady Stanton said, "What will we and our daughters suffer if these degraded black men are allowed to have rights that would make them even worse than our Saxon fathers?" Susan B. Anthony was in on it too. "I will cut off this right arm of mine before I will ever work or demand the ballot for the negro and not the woman." Notice how this statement effectively erased black women from the conversation. When black men were granted the right to vote in 1870, white suffragists were pissed because they believed they were better than black men. Frances

E. Willard said "It is not fair that a plantation Negro who can neither read or write should be entrusted with the ballot," before going on to say black men were dangerous threats to white womanhood. By tapping into white men's fear of nigger rape, Willard hoped to leverage white womanhood for a few male privileges. White women were women, but more importantly (as they implied), they were white.

Ida B. Wells saw through the fake ass Frances and her hateful speech against black men, realizing that she and other white suffragists wanted to gain support from white men who were "hanging, shooting, and burning negroes alive." Frances and other white feminists weren't out hanging, shooting, and burning.... But they were okay with aligning themselves with the men who were. Their reputations of purity allowed them to wreak racial havoc on a dignified pedestal. To Great Britain, Frances Willard was the "uncrowned queen of American democracy", a moral and righteous woman who would never ignore a lynching epidemic. They were quite surprised when Ida B. Wells showed up for a British women's rights convention and read some of Willard's inflammatory speech aloud.

On the same day Donald Trump was elected with 53% of the white woman's vote, feminists gathered at Susan B. Anthony's grave with "I Voted" stickers. A few think-pieces popped up from self-identified feminists who explained why they voted for a man who emboldened white racists. It all echoed the reality of white feminism: "We are women, but we're white first." When forced to choose between retaining racial privilege or fighting sexist oppression, the majority of white women will choose their privilege every time. But even still,   29 they'll always call on black women for numbers if they need them.

Faux-Politically Empowered Girlfriends and Wives

These are the women who gained the right to vote in the 1920s and went buck wild. "White supremacy will be strengthened, not weakened, by women's suffrage," said Carrie Chapman Catt. As the recent election demonstrated, she was right. While the KKK became more popular in the years leading up to The Great Depression, white protestant women joined the WKKK in droves. Many of them joined when or after their husbands did. Like their male counterparts, they believed their rights were being trampled on by black people and immigrants. They were also terrified of the black rapist, a villain perpetuated by the popular 1916 film, *Birth of a Nation*. It shouldn't be shocking that many of these women were former suffragettes. Even though in the present day the KKK's once mighty power has been whittled down to hundreds of smaller hate groups, the women who aligned themselves with these male-dominated arenas are still around. A contemporary version of this white woman is likely to be decked out in confederate flag belts, uses the complete term "the white race" frequently, and potentially has a drug or alcohol problem. She votes however her father/boyfriend/brothers tell her (if she votes in those "rigged zionist abortions" at all, that is), believes white genocide is imminent, and thinks feminism is cancer.

Polite But Still Racist Southern Belles

Ah, a true classic. As a North Carolina native, I have come into contact with a dizzying amount of women like this here in the 21st Century. Well-off white women in costly sundresses with withered french manicured hands encrusted in diamonds; who often clutch at their pearls and say "Bless your heart." They're always polite, but usually haughty. Some of the ones I've come into contact with have praised me for being articulate or pretty as if smart or pretty black girls are a rarity. I pity the black people who had to deal with these phony bitches during the Jim Crow era when their negative opinion could get your house set on fire or your husband strung up from a tree. Hiding behind dainty dresses, southern manners, and the assertion that she treated her negro servants like members of the family, the racist southern belle was a fixture on the 20th-century American landscape.

With a sugary sweet accent, Christian rhetoric, leisurely afternoons spent gossiping and being nosy, and the power of being married to a man that mattered in the eyes of the law, the average southern white woman was an entitled monster. She was fine with negroes as long as they stayed in their place- aka staying subservient to white people. She was also fine with violence against negroes. In *Coming of Age in Mississippi*, Anne Moody recalled her employer, Mrs. Burke, saying that Emmett Till would never have been murdered had he not 'forgot his place'. Mrs. Burke, and thousands of other women like her, blamed the violent behavior of their husbands, brothers, sons, cousins, and neighbors on black people getting out of place. What a convenient way to excuse depravity from the safe haven of white womanhood.

The "I'm a Racist Because I'm a Good Mother" Women

Somebody's child is always being used to justify bullshit. When white parents found out black Ruby Bridges was going to be attending their New Orleans school, they were pissed. One woman, obviously concerned about the 5-year-old Bridges threatening the safety of her own child, threatened to poison Ruby on her daily walks to school. This attitude was repeated by every racist white woman during the integration years. White women being foul racists for the alleged sake of their children was and is common, and made clear by the dozens of unnamed white women you see yelling angrily in historic integration photos. The sadder part? Many have never been identified and never will be.

The Lover of Black Men and Hater of Black Women

This is a relatively new category of white woman, as for the majority of American history miscegenation has been illegal and widely frowned upon. But in the 21st century, this woman thrives. She loves black men and black culture. She publicly applauds black rights. She doesn't say nigga. She's cool. She's down. But at some point, she reveals her true colors and competitive nature. "I love black cock," she says, signifying that her love for black men isn't genuine or loyal but instead founded in fetishism. "Black women hate me because black men love me," she says with total seriousness. Or, "Black girls just mad because they have to wear weave and white girls wear their real hair, THAT'S WHY WE STEALING YOUR MEN." Statements like these blatantly reveal her superiority complex with the black woman; whom she hates for being the black man's counterpart. Clearly, black men are safe from her hatred because they have something she wants- dick and/or validation. Black women though? The mothers, the sisters, the aunts, and the daughters? We're her enemy.

The Pretty Conduit

Let us go back to Rose Armitage real quick. She seemed innocent and normal until you found out she was raised to kidnap and hypnotize black people for the wanton desires of white family members and friends. Even when Chris KNEW that she was a deranged mayonnaise demon escaped from the deepest pits of hell, he couldn't bring himself to choke her to death. He looked down at her pretty face and decided that he couldn't do it. This was one of the scariest parts of the movie to me because it represents America's response to a type of woman who has grown in popularity thanks to the internet and social media. You already know I'm talking about women like Ann Coulter and Tomi Lahren. She says everything the typical white male racist says- but a sweet voice, a conventionally attractive face, and the privilege of femininity that whiteness grants her keeps the virulent racist bimbo from being labeled as one. Her appearance, gender, and feminine qualities appeal to people that white men can't. Because of her appearance and status as a white woman, she is protected by white and black men alike. To them, she is never angry or bitter, just sassy and passionate. To them she is not racist, just speaking "the truth" or her opinion. In fact, some black men shrug off her racism with a sickening resolve: "I'd still fuck."

At the end of the film when Rose thought she saw a cop car, she knew she could snap back into victim mode. Had it been a cop instead of Chris's friend Rod, they'd have seen a bloodied black man looking down on a broken white woman and shot him in a heartbeat. Rose   33 knew she could weave a tale of rape and terror and go on about her life. **Not every white woman sucks**. But every white woman on this list and every white woman in real life has the fake victim card at her disposal. When my former college roommate Elizabeth experienced my reaction to her threat to do me bodily harm, she flipped a switch. She was no longer the vodka-fueled instigator making threats and acting tough. She was suddenly crying in the hallway, inconsolable and weak. This is white womanhood. This is their ultimate privilege. At any moment they can go from agitator or abuser to a delicate and innocent white woman in need of protection from the big scary black. Even worse, not every black man or woman will be fortunate enough to have a friend like Rod to come save them when they've been accused of violence by a white woman, or when they were simply black in the wrong place at the wrong time. Many have been and will continue to be caught in the web of faux innocence, lies, and evil spun by white women.

Perhaps this is why *Get Out* is one of the scariest movies I've ever seen.

White Privilege
(A Guide For Dummies And Skeptics)

I wrote this with venom flowing through my veins. I'm
fed up with the white people I've been seeing float on
my twitter timeline declaring that white privilege 'isn't a
thing'. Because most whites are socialized to not realize
that they have an abundance of privilege not available
to minorities, quite a few of them ardently believe that
white privilege is a myth. This includes the poor ones,
who benefit from their whiteness even if they deny it.
Years of people of color being subservient and sycophan-
tic have made white people weirdly fragile and insulated
from their real ties. But in 2017 I need ya'll to get with
the program.

Here are 15 examples of white privilege.

1) White privilege is the European and white version of history being the center of MANDATORY curriculum in education, often depicting whites as victors, heroes, and innovators. Minority groups and their accomplishments are explored in non-mandatory elective classes or during designated times of the year. They might even get a few chunks of text in large history books that never mention much more than Frederick Douglass, Martin Luther King Jr's promotion of nonviolence, and more recently, Barack Obama's presidency. Little is mentioned about white re-actions to black progress or blatant acts of racism past the death of MLK.

2) White privilege is multiple types of white people being depicted in entertainment and media. As a white person, you can turn on the TV or pop open a magazine and see white people with straight hair, curly hair, red hair, skinny bodies, fat bodies, etc. Your features have historically been worthy of attention, praise, and pay-checks. You see people who look similar to you in all fac-ets of life being proclaimed beautiful. Up until recently, blacks have been barraged with images of white beauty and few images of black beauty. This obviously has had an effect on black people and how they view themselves.

3) White privilege is being able to speak proper English and use fancy vocabulary without being referred to as "uppity", or being told you're "acting white". Because intelligence is automatically attached to whiteness, it is not poked at. Nobody will be surprised to hear proper grammar or million dollar words tumbling from your mouth. You'll also probably never hear "Wow you're so smart," in a tone of utter disbelief.

4) White privilege is getting into an acclaimed universi-

ty or gaining prominent employment, and people say-ing you did so because you deserved it, not because of affirmative action.

5) White privilege is being able to dress like a "thug", listen to "thug" hip-hop music, or use "thug" Ebonics, but not being worried about actually getting called or treated like one by the authorities.

6) White privilege is being able to own a gun (regis-tered or unregistered) and proclaiming you have the right to bear arms without being labeled a thug. You can even walk around with this gun in public places, strapped to your back or on your hip. You probably won't be stopped and frisked for looking like a potential threat, either. If you are examining a gun in Walmart (toy or otherwise), you won't be shot because as a white American citizen, it is your right to bear arms.

7) White privilege is white people's natural hair being deemed professional and okay in the workplace, while black people's natural hair is often deemed unprofes-sional and unkempt. Your hair is the standard that an-other person's hair is judged by. That is privilege, wheth-er you admit it or not.

8) White privilege is believing you have every right to remember and commemorate Pearl Harbor, 9/11, and Taylor Swift lyrics (all atrocities against the American people), but feel like black people should 'get over' slav-ery (an atrocity against blacks) because racism doesn't exist anymore and there was once a black man in the White House. You remember events that disproportion-ately affected YOUR people. Not only do you place these predominantly white tragedies on pedestals, but you 37

expect minorities to disregard their own past traumas while remembering your own. If this wasn't the truth, you'd be just as zealous about remembering events like Indian Removal, the Tuskegee Syphilis Experiments, and the various deaths of victims of police brutality.

9)   White privilege is being able to complain about your treatment in this country without someone telling you to shut up because "For God sakes, the president is white, racism is dead, stop being bitter, stop making excuses, etc." Your grievances are legitimate, but when people of color do it, they are being ungrateful or race-baiting. By telling a black person that their oppression is dramatized or non-existent, you are ignoring the hundreds of years of disadvantages that have influenced attitudes and systems to maintain the status quo of white supremacy, and exercising your privilege.

10)   White privilege is being able to get drunk or rowdy on drugs at public events and nobody will call you savage, a thug, ghetto, or dangerous.

11)   White privilege is feeling trustful of police officers and being reassured by their presence, not scared by it. White privilege is applauding police officers for keeping you safe while ignoring their very long history of terrorizing and targeting black communities. If you're desperate for more information, check out the Department of Justice's report on Chicago area police officers admitting to using unneeded force on black suspects and using racist slurs.

12)   White privilege is believing that made-up names like Heather, Bethany, and Karen are better than equally made-up names like Keisha, Monique, and Ashanti.

(Note: No name under the sun is not made-up. Please stop calling black names made-up like whatever name you're rocking was bestowed upon you by God).

13)   White woman privilege is being able to avoid being called an "Angry White Woman", even if all you do is spew hatred and racist rhetoric.

14)   White privilege is assuming and perpetuating that important social and religious figures- like Jesus Christ, God, and Santa Claus- are factually white. White privilege is also believing that portraying them as any other race or ethnicity is blasphemy. White privilege is getting mad at JK Rowling for approving a black Hermione Granger (a character she created) but seeing nothing wrong with a white man portraying a real human, like Michael Jackson.

15)   White privilege is being able to call The Boston Tea Party, The American Revolution, the displaying of the confederate flag, and raucous street celebrations after the death of Osama Bin Laden 'patriotic', while in the same breath condemning the rioters and protesters of Ferguson as savages.... with a straight face.

Those were just 15 examples that peek behind the veil of white privilege.   didn't even mention the obvious privileges like lack of police profiling and better chances of employment with higher pay. I have had numerous white friends who didn't realize that being apart of the majority has afforded them certain luxuries that other minorities can only dream of... but once I had meaningful conversations when they were willing to be taught, they began to see their privileges. I would love to not feel nervous around cops, people paid and sworn to   39 protect me. I would love for my little black cousins to learn in school that white politicians, social reformists, and businessmen aren't the only American heroes they should be looking up to. I would love for black women to be able to express themselves in the same manner as Ann Cunter and Thomas Lahren without being labeled "angry black bitches". As a white person, you may be wondering what you're supposed to do with all of this privilege. You're probably thinking, "Well I can't just stop being white, Lexi." Of course you can't. The point of making you aware that you are privileged is so that you can do three things:

1.   Stop downplaying the experiences of minorities with statements like "But racism doesn't exist anymore" or claiming that we're all on an equal playing field. Also stop saying that "we should all be equal" when you know that "should" is idealism, not our actual reality.

2.   Share the knowledge that you have gained with other white people so they too can stop downplaying the experiences of minorities

3.   Attempt to extend these privileges to other minorities in your own areas of life… for example, casting minorities in your films if you're a casting director or on the smaller scale, attempting to teach your white children/cousins/siblings that white people weren't the only people who built this country and extending appreciation to other cultures.

Despite this essay, quite a few of you white people will think, "But why would I want to do examine my privilege? It's not my fault I'm privileged! Sucks to suck but I'll keep enjoying my life." By refusing to acknowledge that you have privileges that should be rights for all and that minorities in this country are faced with many disadvantages, you are identifying yourself as part of the problem. You are a racist, who actively wants to enjoy the fruits of a system built on the discrimination and exploitation of others. You cannot deny this. You are the bump under the rug that needs to be smoothed out. Congratulations, you fuck. You are an asshole and a horrible human being. Cheers.

The Cookout Is Canceled

It doesn't take much for a white person to be invited to the cookout. In this fucked up world, a white person doing the bare minimum nets them an invite into our exclusive club. A white boy dancing on beat? Send him an invite. A white girl saying she'd never call her black boyfriend nigger? Tell her to bring some extra plastic cups on the way to the cookout she is now invited to. I get it. The cookout rhetoric incentivizes white people to become allies. It makes them feel welcome and comfortable among us, instead of feeling like clumsy, in-the-way, guilty pests. But to me, there lies the problem. In the fight against racial oppression, white allies do not deserve to feel comfortable. At no point should their comfort be a priority. As a black person in America, I am a thinly veiled second class citizen. No matter how much I move up in this country, I am always aware that just a few generations ago virulent racists lived openly. They approved of lynching, forced subservience, and systematic oppression. White America's sense of entitlement to this country was strengthened by folks who were comfortable doing what was popular. White comfort is not reliable, nor is it conduive to black progression.

In this socio-political atmosphere as more bigots poke their heads out to play, the last thing I want is comfortable white people. Comfortable white people talk more than they listen. Comfortable white people start asking for favors and special treatment. Comfortable white people start feeling entitled to our culture. Comfortable white people come to expect rewards for not being racist, or for appearing less racist than their peers. After all, this is a country that lauds Abraham Lincoln, a staunch white supremacist, as a savior of black people and eradicator of slavery. The same Lincoln who said:

> "I will say then that I am not, nor ever have been in favor of bringing about in any way the social and political equality of the white and black races – that I am not nor ever have been in favor of making voters or jurors of negroes, nor of qualifying them to hold office, nor to intermarry with white people; and I will say in addition to this that there is a physical difference between the white and black races which I believe will forever forbid the two races living together on terms of social and political equality. And inasmuch as they cannot so live, while they do remain together there must be the position of superior and inferior, and I as much as any other man is in favor of having the superior position assigned to the white race."

Despite these words, Lincoln has been invited to the cookout on numerous occasions. He is often pushed as a hero for black people who died for our freedom. Remember when Obama very deliberately chose to be sworn in with Lincoln's bible? The symbolism of the first black president being sworn in using the bible of the purported pro-black Lincoln was overwhelming. Obama was supposed to be continuing the legacy of justice and black progression that Lincoln once embarked on. Lincoln has been mythicized to the point where he is a go-to president for liberals and conservatives alike who want to remind anyone with twitter access that they are not racist. Every Black History Month he is celebrated with more gusto than many black leaders and historical figures. White America enjoys Lincoln and other "progressive for their time" heroes, who straddled the line between being radical and racist, adapting whichever side was the most comfortable at the time. Most white Americans just want comfort. If that means white supremacy, so be it. If that means a spot on the bench if niggas ever took over this country, so be it. If they are actively seeking to end white supremacy, it is not because it is wrong, it is because they want to be invited to the cookout. They want inclusion into black culture and black absolution of whatever guilt they are carrying.

Every step white people take in this movement should be a reminder of the attitudes and behavior of their ancestors. They do not need to be comfortable and forgetful. They do not need to be forgiving of their ancestors. Every step in this movement should also be a reminder to white people that their aid in the fight for racial equality is not a special treat that they should be rewarded for, but just the beginning of a long list of reparations that they fucking owe us. The world needs to be balanced out. We don't need to thank white people with an invitation to the cookout for things we have been doing for them for centuries. Nor do we owe them benefits from the reparations or privileges we are just now receiving. For example, I have a white European benefactor who has generously helped me grow the Intelexual Media brand. He has asked for nothing in return, even with the clear understanding that I only seek to uplift and employ black people when I am fiscally free to do so. For the last few racially charged centuries he and millions like him have benefitted from the exploitation of people of color. As a true ally, he understands that spreading his wealth to marginalized groups is infinitely more helpful than apologies, tweets, or HBO screenplays about the proliferation of white supremacy. And yet? His donations to me, no matter how generous, have not netted him an invitation to the cookout. Nor has his obvious disregard for fanfare or a financial return on his investment in me.

Perhaps the most annoying kind of cookout invitations are the ones sent out to white people indulging in black culture. Are we so starved for white acceptance and comfort that we reward them for doing things we can do ourselves? Why does a white person doing something culturally black hold so much value to the most gullible in our community? It's incredible that a white person dancing, singing, rapping, or creating with black cultural influences can get shown boundless amounts of love on social media. For example, please tell me the White Australian Rapper Who Shall Remain Unnammed blew up faster than black American female rappers? There are people who will read this and think that I'm taking a phrase (and now prominent feature of meme culture) too seriously. But nah, this mirrors real life. Invita-   45 tions are sent with the hopes that they will be accepted. Too many of us want to make a space for white people because we crave their validation. This is thanks to social conditioning. Subconsciously, many of us get validation from white people indulging in our culture and taking it mainstream because whiteness adds credibility.

In the past, respectability politics called for assimilation into white culture. This meant adopting white culture to not appear threatning or dangerously ethnic (with various results). Despite this, black Americans have forged a culture. It wasn't always celebrated in public spaces (because White society wouldn't approve), but it was ours. In the shadows of our assimilation were white people who liked what we created. When white people like something, it's okay. When I was a blogger in the entertainment industry aspiring young rappers always told me they knew they'd be set when white people became fans. White acceptance brings validation.

Was there ever a time that white people willingly invited niggas to their cookouts? Was there ever a time where our comfort was catered to? Nah. We bled (and still bleed) for freedom, rights, and safety. They didn't just hand it to us. Extending cookout invitations to Hannah, Becky, Susan, Brad, Brock, and Connor for enjoying our culture or saying something we already say? That shit canceled.

Lynch TV

I would say I've seen enough dead black bodies on my social media timelines, but that implies that there was ever a time when I hadn't seen enough. My first peek at an unarmed black person's slaughtered body was in 2012. Trayvon Martin was in full rigor mortis, and there he was on my timeline being retweeted like a sensational twerk video or a compelling plate of food. This was the same time "Long Live Zimmerman" was spray painted on the side of the black student union at the school I was set to attend that Fall. I saw Mike Brown's body lay in the street, swelling from the heat as cops refused to allow medics on the scene. I watched Eric Garner struggle to breathe as his life was stolen from him over untaxed cigarettes. I watched Tamir Rice die

47

in the blink of an eye. More recently, I watched Philando Castille bleed out in front of his girlfriend and child. With each video or image retweeted onto my timeline, I became both a little more numb and a little more motivated. I'm tired of watching clear-cut cases of murder go unpunished, yet I'm motivated to spark the same rage I feel into others in my community.

"I wanted the world to see what they did to my baby." Mamie Till Mobley said when asked why she allowed an open casket funeral for her son Emmett Till. The boy was 14-years-old when his mother sent him off for a summer in Money, Mississippi with relatives. Emmett was stocky and had a reputation for stylish outfits around his Chicago neighborhood. He was just an average boy before he became a historical martyr. Before Mamie said her final goodbye to her only son, she gave him advice on dealing with white people in Mississippi. "Don't hesitate to humble yourself. Even if you have to get on your knees." Her advice was highly necessary. Mississippi was (and still is) the poorest state in the country with the largest black population. It was also one of the most virulently racist places for black people, as over 500 lynchings had been recorded in the state since 1865. It was a different kind of environment for a city boy like Emmett.

On August 25th, 1955, Emmett and his cousins went to Bryant's Grocery and Meat Market for candy. The store, frequented by black sharecroppers in the area, was owned by 24-year old-Roy Bryant and his 21-year-old wife Carolyn. Emmett was alone in that store with Carolyn Bryant for less than a minute. What happened inside has been re-hashed for over half a century. Some said he wolf-whistled at the married white woman. Others, going on Carolyn's fraudulent claim, believed that Emmett had grabbed the woman by her wrist and made a sexual advance. There was even talk of a dare from Emmett's cousins to get fresh with Carolyn. But according to the most credible accounts, Emmett did nothing malicious or threatening to Carolyn Bryant. Moments after exiting the store, Emmett and his cousin Simeon Wright saw Carolyn go out to her car for a gun. Black men at a near-by checker game heard what happened and urged the boys to leave. Emmett was spooked and told his cousin he wanted to go home to Chicago. He would never get to.

On the morning of August 28th, Carolyn's husband and brother in law busted into the home where Emmett was staying and demanded to speak to "the nigger who did the talking." Three days later the naked, bloated, and mutilated body of Emmett Till was found floating in the Tallahatchie River. In addition to a vicious beating that caused his eyeball to pop out, the 14-year-old had been shot in the head. When Mamie Till-Mobley saw her son, he was unrecognizable. "There was just no way I could describe what was in that box. No way. And I wanted the world to see," she explained. This initially had not been easy, as Mississippi authorities sneakily prepared Emmett's body for immediate burial upon discovery. But Mamie refused to be swindled. The story picked up heat in newspapers around the region. The Jackson Daily News and Vicksburg Evening Post both published a picture of Mamie and Emmett from the previous Christmas. While that brought sympathy from whites in the area, it was the photos of disfigured Emmett's face in Jet Magazine and the Chicago Defender that rocked the nation.

In 1955, there were no viral videos, memes, social

media, or internet. And yet, tens of thousands of people saw Emmett's mangled body at the funeral. Millions more saw pictures of it in magazines. Though Emmett's murderers would go free (and later brag about killing the fourteen-year-old boy), the incident forced many Americans to acknowledge the widespread and seldom punished act of lynching. Though a vigilante tradition that dated back to the 18th century, Mamie Hill Mobley personalized a common tragedy and returned humanity to lynch victims.

Lynchings came to prominence with the increased circulation of newspapers in the 19th century. From 1875 to 1920, papers reported on them with chilling detail, chewing through these indecencies with nonchalance or praise. The sight of bloodied and burnt black bodies became commonplace with the wider availability of cameras in the 20th century. There are photos of smiling white faces underneath their victims, stamped onto postcards. At least 81 lynching photos survive today. While lynchings were terrible ordeals for black people, to many whites the act of violence was a benign aspect of American culture. Despite the popular adage "innocent until proven guilty" and the fact that lynching was vigilantism, the alleged crimes of victims were usually listed in the article to squash any potential sympathy in readers. Lynch victims were spun as savage brutes, while their murderers were turned into heroes and praised for doing what others couldn't or wouldn't do. Sound familiar? This was a particularly true narrative in the South, where lynching was believed to be a natural part of the racial order.

In a 1920 Florida newspaper named *The Ocala Evening Star*, a man named W.E. Wimpy from Clarkston, Georgia defended an earlier criticism of lynching culture as a "weakness of the county government that didn't happen in strong cities.' He called for the end of lynching. Readers of the paper sent hate mail that included the line "For a southern man, Mr. Wimpy is careless." The editor of the paper berated Wimpy, claiming that lynching kept black people in line and white women safe. "In these southern states life and property are safer than in many other parts of the world," he boasted. "A careful analysis will show that women are safer in the south than elsewhere. Once in awhile, a brutal negro will commit an outrage on a white woman, and be visited with summary vengeance." The paranoia of protecting white women from black rapists radiated throughout the South and gave lynching a false righteousness. It was easy to shrug away lynching when you believed it was done for public safety. But in truth, most black men were not lynched because of rape allegations. We know this thanks to Ida B. Wells.

After the 1892 murders of three of her friends, Ida began investigating the prevalence of lynching. She raised $500 (nearly $13,000 in today's money) and set to work. Before her investigation, she believed the act of rape justified lynch mobs. In an eerie echo of "black on black crime" arguments made by misinformed opponents of Black Lives Matter, Ida once wrote: "although lynching was...contrary to law and order...it was the terrible crime of rape [that] led to the lynching; [and] that perhaps...the mob was justified in taking his [the rapist's] life." After her research, Ida found that black men were mostly lynched for voting or running for political office. She realized that the black on white rape myth was employed not only by whites but also by upper-class blacks who preferred to turn a blind eye to lynching. Ida decided to publish a pamphlet, *Southern Horrors: Lynch Law in All Its Phases*. Three years after, she published *The Red Record*, a pamphlet documenting cases of lynching since 1863. She noted that lynching had risen once whites no longer saw freed black people as economically valuable property.

Criticizing and analyzing lynching was not common. Racist whites seethed with hatred at Ida, but her pamphlets served their purpose of educating the community. Anti-lynch fervor grew (as lynching itself intensified during the nadir of American race relations) but still, the government did little. 1919 was a particularly bad year for lynching. At least 25 "race riots" occurred during 1919, also known as the year of Red Summer. The biggest incident of mass murder that year took place in Little Rock, Arkansas when 237 black sharecroppers were hunted down by hundreds of white men, most of them war veterans.

In the 1920s, the attitude towards lynching slightly shifted as more papers became less permissive of the act. The NAACP started to press for anti-lynching legislation, thanks to influence from black World War One vets who had come home from the war especially fed up with American racism. But the turbulence of the Great Depression and World War II put racial issues on the backburner. Lynching still happened, with few interjections from White America. To most whites, the black criminals who were lynched were not actual humans. There was no reason for pity, outrage, or calls for legislation. So when Emmett Till's bloated and disfigured face was printed in close proximity to that of his grieving mother, some white Americans placed themselves in her shoes. By broadcasting her pain and the murder of her son, Mamie catalyzed the Civil Rights Movement and officially besmirched the heroic reputation of lynching in America. Even though Mamie and Emmett's story sparked outrage, the two murderers, Roy Bryant and J.W. Milam, were not convicted. Even still, Emmett and Mamie sparked a turning point in lynch culture. After a lot of blood, sweat, and tears from those inspired and angered by Mamie's pain, anti-lynching legislation was passed thirteen years later.

Today, the sight of unjustly murdered black people and their inconsolable relatives doesn't cause as much of a stir as Mamie Till Mobley did. It's a repugnant reality. If we didn't see these murders on social media or TV, we'd be clueless about them. But because we do see them, we're becoming desensitized. It is the extra gruesome murders that get airtime and speculation on TV, where news networks use black snuff films for ratings. But ratings do not equal justice. Dead black bodies at the hands of police get attention, but not guilty verdicts. This 24/7 channel of black pain is a fear tactic. Brutalization of black bodies is normalized and unpunished, numbing many of us to any idea of revolution.

"That's how it's always been," we have all said at one point, feeling so helpless about the state of black lives in America that permanently tracing in awareness on the issues for Love and Hip Hop and other ignorant fun sounds palatable. With each video, we are reminded that lynching is still alive in 2017. With each video, we are forced to think of the untold number of black people murdered by a racist when there were no cameras around. With each video, we are forced to think about the names that go unsaid and the murder investigations that go un-pressed because the victim wasn't "spe-   53 cial" enough to warrant viral attention.

I have seen dozens of images and videos of black people shot, choked, or beaten to death by cops or vigilantes who later claimed that they feared for their lives. I have seen news outlets suggest that victims deserved their deaths, while simultaneously handling murderers like Dylan Roof and James Holmes with kid gloves. I have seen the same public figures who share police brutality murders like jolly ranchers spit outrage at the autopsy photos of Robin Williams. I watch, even when I don't want to. Some people can close their eyes. Some people can scroll right past triggering videos on their timeline. But not me. I need to see. I need to be reminded why my rage at this country is legitimate. For me, there is no remote. there is no escaping.

Fuck The Pledge of Allegiance

I don't remember the exact moment that I began questioning the pledge but it was fifth grade when I started refusing to put my hand over my heart and recite those loaded words. The phrase "I pledge allegiance" felt sticky and wrong in my mouth. At first, I stopped saying the words. Then, I stopped standing up altogether. My fifth-grade teacher, a stern middle-aged blonde who often showed contempt towards me did not approve. She pulled me aside before recess and demanded that I say the pledge of allegiance, or that she would be forced to call my mother. She did not ask me why I refused to say the pledge. She just wanted to make sure that I said it. She, like many, assumed that a ten-year-old should pledge her unwavering loyalty to a country while

55

knowing very little about it.

The American Pledge of Allegiance has been around in various forms since 1892 when Colonel George Balch yearned to teach American loyalty to children. He was especially keen on kick-starting American nationalism in the children of immigrants. His original words were 'we give our heads and hearts to God and our country; one country, one language, one flag!' Five years after Balch, Francis Bellamy tweaked the pledge for a special edition issue of the popular children's magazine *The Youth's Companion*. The pledge was going to be used to commemorate the 400th anniversary of Christopher Columbus's arrival. The official words were now 'I pledge allegiance to my Flag and the Republic for which it stands, one nation, indivisible, with liberty and justice for all.' It was accompanied by the Bellamy Salute, the same gesture adopted by Nazi Germany decades later. Bellamy had considered including the word "equality" in the pledge, but he knew that opponents of blacks, indigenous people, and women wouldn't want to recite those words.

The American flag was commercialized for public schools at the same time, and the flag observing ceremony was pushed by Bellamy and the National Education Association. In June 1892, they succeeded in persuading President Benjamin Harrison into making the pledge, salute, and flag the center of Columbus Day. On October 12, 1892, students across the nation pledged their loyalty to America for the first time. Many schools eventually made the pledge a required part of the school day.

In June 1942, during the turbulence of World War II, the

pledge was officially adopted by Congress. This was the same year that roughly 70,000 Japanese-Americans were rounded up and tossed into internment camps. The pledge, which called for liberty and justice for all, reeked of hypocrisy. In the ten years prior, a quiet war had been brewing between Jehovah's Witnesses and advocates of the pledge. In Nazi Germany, thousands of Jehovah's Witnesses were arrested for not saluting the swastika stamped flag. To show solidarity, some American Jehovah's Witnesses instructed their children to abandon America's pledge. The responses weren't pleasant. Students were suspended or expelled and threatened with reform school. Parents were arrested. Some Jehovah's Witnesses even experienced violence.

In 1940 the Supreme Court ruled that public school students could be compelled to say the pledge, no matter their religion. Not saying the pledge was considered an act of insubordination. This was overturned in 1943's *West Virginia State Board of Education vs Barnette*. The Supreme Court ruled that the free speech clause in the 1st amendment protected students from being forced to salute the flag or say the pledge. Today, saying the pledge of allegiance is optional, but students still get harassed for not saying it. For instance, it was reported a few months ago that a Michigan sixth grader was "violently snatched out of his chair and made to stand" after exercising his right to free speech. On a separate occasion, he was yelled at.

My fifth-grade teacher was disgusted when I stopped saying the pledge. She thought I was making trouble. After all, it was only three years after 9/11 and American nationalism was at a fever pitch. There is a lot of confusing language used to describe that era. If you   57 ask the wrong person, they'll call that era patriotic. But George Orwell defined patriotism as "devotion to a particular place and a particular way of life, which one believes to be the best in the world but has no wish to force on other people." On the flip side, he described nationalism as feeling your way of life or country is superior to others and should be adopted by everyone. In the months and years after the 9/11 attacks, sales of flags increased but so did the feelings of xenophobia and nationalism. Americans oozed love for country and grew fervently opposed to those they saw as "other". Attacks on Middle Eastern and Muslim Americans increased to never before seen levels. The violent criminals who attacked them were publicly shamed but then heralded as heroes and patriots on right-wing blogs and forums. It was this twisted nationalism that fueled the average citizen's belief that we should incite war in the Middle East. Additionally, there are essays and entire books that can be written about the link between post-9/11 American nationalism and the presidential election of Donald Trump.

Despite my teacher's warning, I continued to not stand for the pledge. She followed through with her threat to call my mother, and I'm sure that she was thoroughly surprised when my mother stood behind my decision. I can only imagine what kind of rebuke she handed down to my dear teacher, who after that call never asked me to stand for the pledge again. For the rest of the year, she always addressed me with the utmost respect, albeit her eyes were always two or three inches above my head as if she was afraid to look me in the eye. What my teacher didn't grasp was that when she rebuked my decision she was denying me access to liberty and justice, a core component of the pledge she was so desperate for me to say. Even with my naive understanding of the world at the age of ten, I knew she was wrong. Thirteen years later, I can articulate that America is also wrong for dipping children into blind allegiance before they ever have the inclination to question it. There is a danger in making American kids think that this country does a thorough job at extending liberty and justice to all of its citizens, no matter their race, religion, gender, or socio-economic status.

The concept of the pledge would be less terrifying if it wasn't such blatant propaganda. The words of the pledge are absorbed in kindergarten when the mind is young and malleable. As your vocabulary expands, the words become more familiar. As the years go by, the assurances of justice and liberty for all are validated by shallow American history lessons that skip past geno-cide, the most brutal aspects of chattel slavery, mass sterilization, and systematic oppression. Set adrift on manipulated memory bliss of American atrocities, the pledge becomes righteous and sacred. The flag, truly a symbol of imperialism, theft, genocide, and injustice-becomes more important than the things it's supposed to represent. You know, like justice, liberty, and equality for all. Have you ever noticed that conservatives and liberals alike get angrier about a burning flag than police brutality, housing discrimination, or other components of white supremacy? These are the same people who see valid critiques of America's racial issues as blasphemous or blown out of proportion. They are essentially ren-dered incapable of revolution. They have no desire to re-vise this country's race relations or balance its economic inequalities. Why? They are brainwashed into unyielding support of a country that has sanitized its past for gen-erations of school children.   59

On Zombies and the Audacity of American History Curriculum

Apart from a few ridiculous cinematic renditions, the life of a zombie is a pretty simple one. It craves human flesh, no matter the peril or risk at hand. It lumbers about aimlessly until an opportunity for flesh presents itself. Skin rips and body parts fall off due to incessant wandering, but no lessons are learned. The zombie mind is impenetrable to new knowledge. It only knows chewing flesh, walking, and how to hear things. Its ignorance of its surroundings and reality dooms it to detriment at the hands of a human, in the crossfire of warring groups, or by accident over a cliff. It simply exists until it dies. Zombies do not stop to think about why they're zombies or even what happens if they eat all the humans and animals.

As higher education is often out of reach for those who can't afford it, public school is commonly the only formal learning experience for a significant swath of American children. Through a complex system resting on racism, classism, and capitalism, the bulk of these institutions churn out zombie citizens. Think of the people you know who mindlessly chew through America's accomplishments, atrocities, and apologies with unwavering loyalty and without question. They ignore contradictions about our country like bipartisanship cults and the illusion of democracy and still utter "land of the free" despite the realities of mass incarceration. They glorify the few American wars they can identify as fights for our freedom, not conflicts of greed and genocide. Reputable sources and profanity-laced lectures do not penetrate their irrevocable patriotism.They are perfect citizens, who allow this country's acts of tyranny to go unpunished and unexamined. None of this is an accident. American K-12 curriculum is built to enforce the racial hierarchy, weaken democracy, and make us all good slaves blind to the worst parts of capitalism.

In 1763 Frederick the Great introduced compulsory education for all boys and girls in Prussia from the age of 5. While designed to increase literacy, the Prussian education system was also meant to teach obedience and loyalty. By the 1830's the system was a beacon of innovation to other countries. America's few schools were riddled with problems, and a former politician turned education reformer named Horace Mann wanted to fix this. While working as the secretary of the Massachusetts Board of Education, Mann studied school systems from various countries and settled on the

Prussian Model. Among his chief education concerns were "the public should no longer remain ignorant" and "education should be paid for, controlled, and sustained by an interested public." His most important idea, however, was that schools be secular. He wanted them to emphasize the importance of literacy and obedience to authority without all the religious hoopla. Parents agonized over leaving the moral education of their children to teachers and Mann was met with resistance, but it didn't last. Within six decades, schools across the country were following his model.

In 1916, educator Ellwood Cubberly described the role of Americans schools was "to break up these groups or settlements [of children], to assimilate and amalgamate these people as part of our American race, and to implant in their children so far as can be done, the Anglo-Saxon conception of righteousness, law and order and popular government." This was the common attitude about education, and it reflected in the curriculum where white history was centralized and prioritized. While a lot has changed about our country since the 19th century when Mann first decided that daily six to eight-hour blocks in a classroom were the best way to educate the youth, our schools have not. Efficiency and creating productive citizens remain the two priorities while critical thinking remains an elusive skill. Real history also remains missing from many classrooms. We can thank Texas for that.

Everything is bigger in Texas, including the textbook orders. As the 2nd largest state and the number one buyer of textbooks, the Texas State Board of Education can and does encourage publishers to add or omit certain details or refuse to order. For instance, in 1994 the board requested 400 changes in five health books, some of which included omitting LGBT support groups and suicide prevention toll-free numbers. But Texas's biggest influence is revisionist American history. Ever wondered why so many so many Americans are clueless about government blunders and racism? It is estimated that roughly 50-80% of history textbooks approved by Texas are used in other states. The real kick? Those textbooks are approved by just FIFTEEN people. Almost all of them are conservatives and almost none of them are qualified to curate curriculum. Several members throughout the last two decades have publicly disavowed evolution, unpleasant racist realities, secularism, modern science, and support for non-heterosexual youth.

In 2010, Texas's social studies curriculum was up for review. America had a black president. The state board clearly had two goals on the menu: brainwashing and erasure. They claimed to be fighting back against liberal bias in a number of ways. In addition to shooting down the notion of examining the concept of separation and state in-depth, they denied an amendment that required students to study how the founding fathers advocated against favoring one religion over any other. The board also voted to promote the upsides of slavery, including approving a book that called slaves workers. The board furthered their agenda by saying that the Civil War should be taught as a battle for states rights while also heroizing Jefferson Davis. They even decided to keep ignoring most black and Latino history, while emphasizing the violence of the Black Panthers and the pacifism of Martin Luther King Jr. as mutually exclusive.

In 2012, the Republican Party of Texas denounced the teaching of critical thinking skills. Three years later, 63 the Texas State Board of Education rejected a measure that would require university experts to fact check textbooks. The cycle of misinformation and ignorance is likely to continue because Texas consistently has the 2nd to lowest voter turnout in the country. The State Board of Education is filled with wealthy and conservative elected officials brainwashed from the last generation of faulty textbooks and ideas, who then push their views on the youth. The conservatism of Texas is reinforced each generation by direct brainwashing at the hands of the state's board of education.

The current members of the Texas State Board of Education who decide how and what children in the most populated place in the country were around for reactions to curriculum reform in the 70s. It was 1974 when conservative parents in West Virginia rioted upon learning that students would be learning black history. The ringleader, Kanawha County School Board member Alice Moore, said that the 300 books approved by the state were "filthy, disgusting, trash, unpatriotic, and unduly favoring blacks." Her words set off a boycott of the schools that even brought about three bombings (on two schools and a school board building) and drive-bys on busses. The books were still implemented the next year. This further alienated conservative Americans in the aftermath of the progressive 60s, and private Christian schools became popular.

This brings me to another problem with the state of American education. A growing portion of our population is receiving highly racist and misinformed Christian educations via private schools and homeschooling. Every year roughly 1,770,000, or 3.4% of American youths, are homeschooled. Experts say that number has been growing at a rate of 3-8% a year since 2012. 68% of these students are white, compared to 15% Hispanic, 8% black, and 4% of Asian/Pacific Islanders. 36% of these white students are receiving tailored Christian educations from curriculum publishers like Accelerated Christian Education, Christian Library Academy School System, and Bob Jones University Press. Bob Jones University is famously racist and fought to keep black students off of their campus well into the 1980s. As for the Accelerated Christian Education, they omit most of the Civil Rights Movement except for rioting after the assassination of Martin Luther King Jr. Of course, unbridled racism isn't the only form of bigotry encouraged in some homeschools. As one blogger put it when discussing the pros of homeschooling, "...But no matter what standard you are setting for them in the home, if you send your kids to government schools, they eventually will come home speaking excitedly about gender fluidity, racial privilege, microaggressions, environmental justice, and cultural appropriation."

That writer is extremely optimistic about public schools. A lot of public schools don't ever offer personal finance courses, let alone sociology geared courses. Recall Ellwood Cubberly's quote on the role of public education. He and others believed schools should teach assimilation, American pride, and obedience. Cultivating intelligence, intra-cultural empathy, and critical thinking skills were not mentioned.

When Texas re-examined and updated its social studies curriculum in 2010 it did so with the clear goal of creating citizen zombies. Citizens who are not being taught to critically think and challenge their government to do what it was created for. In Texas, where voter turnout is not only pathetically low but also Republican, this matters. Money runs Texas schools. If money disproportionately belongs to white men who are against ending wealth disparity, voter disenfranchisement, and mass incarceration, how the fuck do you think they're educating the children? Now take Texas's cycle of brainwashing and place it on the national stage.

During the 2016 election season and the months that followed Trump's appointment to the presidency, it became radically clear how foolish and gullible people are in this country. The popularity of maliciously erroneous "news" platforms like Fox News, Infowars, and Breitbart show that a lot of our schools are doing a shitty job of teaching critical thinking and source verification. It has become too easy for people to eschew facts and logic in favor of opinions and misinformation that fits their twisted worldviews. They are infected with ignorance.

Most zombie fiction avoids detailing the source or origin of all the mayhem. Bypassing the frequent origin prediction of bio-weapon gone awry, I place my money on some gnarly genius sociopath hell-bent on destroying the human race because he got denied by his top choice art school (or whatever). At the outbreak, we were all expected to turn zombie or resign ourselves to a similar fate with a shotgun blast to the face. But instead, some of us fought back. We resisted. Some of us survive. We see the zombies and not only hate them but pity them. How do you tell a zombie that it's a zombie? You don't. In the genre, you either try to run from it or kill it. But then there is always that one foolishly naive survivor who thinks they can cure zombies. As I watch millions of my fellow citizens mill about life without questioning the system (or ever seeking to challenge it), I struggle with the constant desire to educate them or wash my hands of them. Are they irreparably damaged, or is there a cure somewhere out there? Is there a way to reach people who have been infected with ignorance? No matter what I choose they'll attack me as I act, like a horde of zombies surrounding me, attempting to drag me down in their ranks.

The Sticky Relationship Between Evangelism, Racism, and American Schools

In February 1956, the pastor of the largest congregation in the Southern Baptist Convention, W.A. Criswell, stood before a sea of white Christians in Dallas, Texas and denounced integration as "idiocy". Seething with anger at black churches and the NAACP, he called them "two by scathing good for nothing fellows who are trying to upset all of the things that we love as good old southern people and as good old southern baptists." The crowd of good southern baptists roared with applause as Criswell joked "In heaven, we'll all be together." Those six words reveal an ugly and complex truth about the relationship between evangelism and racism in this country, even over 70 years after they were uttered. Those six words illustrate that too many white Christians believe there is only room for equality and retrospect in the afterlife... but now is not the time. Five years after his scathing anti-integration speech, Criswell would claim Africans and their descendants were cursed by God to be servant people. The Hamitic myth was a common utterance from white Christians throughout the civil rights movement. While things like this aren't usually said out loud anymore, the concept of black inferiority remains prevalent among evangelicals. The proof is in the schools.

A common misconception about the conservative religious right is that they were drawn together and empowered to political action after *Roe vs Wade* in 1973. Actually, it was not abortion that triggered white evangelicals, but integration. While black leaders—both religious and secular— celebrated forced desegregation in the 1960s, white leaders recoiled. Said Jerry Falwell Sr: "If Chief Justice Warren and his associates had known God's word and had desired to do the Lord's will I am quite confident that the 1954 decision would never have been made... the facilities should be separate. When God has drawn a line of distinction, we should not attempt to cross that line...the true negro does not want integration... he realizes his potential is far better among his own race.... [Integration] will destroy our race eventually. In one northern city, a pastor friend of mine tells me that a couple of opposite race live next door to his church as man and wife."

Despite *Brown*, white leaders saw a loophole. The ruling of *Brown vs Board* did not apply to private schools. White parents began yanking their children out of public schools in droves. By 1974, roughly half a million white students were taken out of school. Industrious white investors erected private schools (aka segregation academies), where admission was limited to the right kind of student. In 1959, Prince Edward County of Virginia 69 closed all their public schools for five years to spite the black population. While most black students in the area didn't get to attend school, white students were enrolled at private academies.

Across the country, non-catholic Christian schools doubled enrollments between 1961 and 1971 and then doubled again over the following ten years. Jerry Falwell Sr. himself founded Liberty Christian Academy in 1967. Pamphlets enticed parents with promises of curriculum laced with "traditional values" and anti-liberal rhetoric. Historian Jason Sokol noted, "[Christian school] supporters wanted to create a world where racial tensions did not exist, so they built schools where racial differences had no place."

These schools promised parents that black students wouldn't be around to ruin their child's education. To make matters worse, the educations provided in these schools indoctrinated students into white supremacy by downplaying or neglecting the role of minorities in America. Other schools promoted archaic ideas about scientific racism and evolution. Because these schools rejected government interference on religious grounds, they were allowed to run their schools as they saw fit. Unfortunately, bigotry was on the agenda. To make matters worse, because these schools were created as faith-based institutions, they could claim tax-exempt status. These schools became profitable.

In 1969, after black parents in Mississippi initiated a lawsuit to stop three private white only schools from getting tax exempt status, the IRS created a policy denying tax exemptions to segregated schools. The thinking was that discriminatory schools can't be charitable, and therefore shouldn't be tax exempt. Schools and leaders reacted. Bob Jones University staunchly informed the IRS that it did not accept blacks. The IRS warned them to integrate, so Bob Jones University admitted one black student, who dropped out after a month. In 1975 they admitted blacks, but only if they were married. This was to discourage interracial dating. The IRS wasn't pleased, and Bob Jones University lost tax-exempt status in 1976. This sent a shockwave through the evangelical community. Enter Paul Weyrich, a conservative political activist. Determined to turn evangelicals into a consolidated voting group, Weyrich had previously tried to use "porn, prayer in schools, the proposed equal rights amendment to the constitution [and] even abortion." But nothing would stick until he got evangelicals to rally around keeping their schools nigger-free.

The Moral Majority political organization was founded in 1979 by Jerry Falwell Sr., born from evangelical rage at "intervention against Christian schools." They threw their support behind Ronald Reagan, abandoning the Democrat Jimmy Carter who allowed the IRS to intervene at their schools. Only after this movement began did the Christian right also decide to target abortion, which had largely been a Catholic issue through the 70s. In fact, southern baptists were encouraged to work for abortion legislation at the Southern Baptist Conventions in 1971, 1974, and 1976. Abortion issues suddenly became tied into the same neat package as "family values", which also encompassed anti-miscegenation. "Family values" was something private schools could advocate for without sounding super racist. In 1980, Ronald Reagan called out the IRS's "unconstitutional regulatory agenda" against independent schools. In 1982, the Reagan administration said it would defend 71

Bob Jones University and its racial policies, citing family values. After minor outrage, Reagan backed off and said the courts would decide. The supreme court disagreed with Reagan's stance, ruling against Bob Jones University 8-1 in 1983. The one person to vote in favor of Bob Jones University, William Rehnquist, was promoted to Chief Justice of the Supreme Court by Reagan in 1986. Ronald Reagan also appointed Robert Billings, the Moral Majority's first executive director, to the Department of Education.

In 2016, 81% of white evangelicals voted for Donald Trump. They initially rallied around him when he made his political mark by accusing Obama of not being an American citizen. A group that prides itself on so-called family values elected a man who lies routinely, owned casinos, cheated on his wife, has been married multiple times and admitted to sexually assaulting women. Jerry Falwell Jr, who inherited his father's Liberty University as well as his unbridled racism, was asked to lead a task force on higher education by Trump in January. He has indicated that he finds the federal law banning discrimination in education as "burdensome." Next, Trump nominated Betsy DeVos to be Secretary of Education, which delighted his evangelical supporters. Why? DeVos is a major promoter of school choice, in which parents are given vouchers to send their students off to private schools if they don't want to be enrolled in public schools. The problem? First, vouchers don't cover the full cost of tuition, rendering them virtually useless to low-income students. Secondly, the number of predominately white private schools with discriminatory admission policies is growing, just like the percentage of segregated schools. With the Trump administration, there is a guarantee that this will operate unchecked.

Time and time again, white parents have shown that if given the choice, they prefer to have their children enrolled at white schools. This wouldn't be a problem if those schools didn't have better resources than public schools that minorities are corralled into or if they didn't promote white supremacy.... but they do.

In the present, 43% of private Christian schools have student bodies that are over 90% white. These schools offer sugarcoated views of history that purposely avoid guilt or retrospection on American race relations, creating legions of white students who are incapable of seeing institutional racism for the true beast that it is. Ever look around and wonder why so many white teens in 2017 say bigoted things straight out of the 1950s? You can blame their parents and their shitty educations.

I've been asked numerous times why segregated schools are a big deal. The issue is that segregated schools operate on the basis of "separate but equal", a wholly unattainable fallacy. Black students are more likely to attend low-income schools that are predominately black, which can affect their future. Per *The Atlantic*, "Data is available for African American students in 97 large cities. In 83 of those 97 cities (or 85.6 percent), the majority of African American students attends schools where most of their classmates qualify as poor or low income. In 54 of those cities, at least 80 percent of black students attend schools where most of their classmates qualify as poor or low-income." In that same article, "Researchers have found that the single-most powerful predictor of racial gaps in educational achievement is the extent to which students attend schools surrounded by other low-income students." Basically? Going to poor schools and being surrounded by poor people does not pro- 73 mote success. Segregated schools are problematic for everyone, and will only continue to flourish while white evangelical Christians refuse to address racism amongst their own.

"In heaven, we'll all be together" was an easy cop out for W.A. Criswell. But it is an ideology— equality would come in the afterlife—that permeated the thinking of blacks and whites before he even uttered the words in 1956. When the tortured slave snuck off at night to worship in secret, the thought of the afterlife stayed with him or her. There wouldn't be salvation in their lifetime but in the next. Think of the highly popular song of the civil rights movement, *Oh Freedom*. "Before I'd be a slave, I'll be buried in my grave, and go home to my lord and be free," marchers would sing through tear gas and mayhem. When blacks have yearned for freedom this meant desiring full social, political, and economic equality to whites. In the song, freedom comes in death. If they don't get what they're asking for in their lifetime- equality, safety, peace- they'll get it in death. As any 20th-century black pastor would tell you, in heaven, there would be no hierarchy. God loves all of his creations equally. But if racist white evangelicals had it their way, heaven would be divided into two separate segments. Just like the school system.

What's God Got to Do With It?
[Christianity & Capitalism]

Few things annoy me more than hearing a wealthy person call their fortune the result of being "blessed" or "highly favored". First, it implies that God has an exclusive and mysterious category of favorites that poor people aren't apart of. For the record, there are roughly 45 million Americans living below the poverty line. Millions of non-Americans are even poorer. Secondly, the language around wealth and blessings mistakenly claims that God bestows wealth on people as a reward for their faith- not because of privilege, circumstance, or back door bargaining. While people sell sex, deadly drugs, or scam to survive, somewhere a rich person sits, believing that God blessed them with obscene amounts of money that others weren't worthy of. They kick back and believe that they are winners of capitalism because God willed it, ignoring the systematic restraints placed on the losers. A strong problem with this way of thinking? If you believe God the Almighty blesses people with money because they are good and faithful, you must also believe that all rich people are good, and deserve what they have.

There is no sentence scathing enough to describe the bloodcurdling laugh that escapes from my throat at the thought of every rich person being righteous enough for God's material blessings. I could easily fill a thick volume with the insidious crimes and corruption of the wealthy, but there is no need. I won't torture you with statistics for the light penalties of white collar crimes or the impact of wealth on public perception. Instead, I'll just ask you to think about who is currently in the White House (and who helped put him there). Too often the wealthy are allowed to escape punishment for deeds that poorer people would never be able to disentangle themselves from. The attachment of holiness and goodness to wealth creates a layer of protection around people whose money already affords them legal, financial, political, and social security. But this is no accident.

When the founding fathers developed the Treaty of Tripoli in 1797, they made it clear that "the government of the United States of America is not, in any sense, founded on the Christian religion." Despite how it may appear, America was founded without an official religion, making it secular. But is it really? On the back of your dollar bills are four words unbefitting of a secular nation. Those four words reveal an appalling truth about the relationship between Christianity and capitalism on American soil. Interestingly, this is the same soil where many people hold tightly to the notion that our founding fathers believed all citizens have a fundamental right to own guns. The nation's secularism is conditional.

Guns, however, are not. While both Jesus and greed are as American as the term "thoughts and prayers" in the wake of a mass shooting, the connection between worship and wealth was not made explicitly clear until the mid-1930s in response to Roosevelt's New Deal. In fact, it was marketed as a mainstream ideology by America's wealthiest.

Because the goals of the New Deal involved stabilizing the economy, providing employment, and reforming businesses so that the Great Depression would never happen again, you'd think that everyone would have loved the concept. Alas, big businesses and the people who owned them despised the New Deal. They weren't happy with government meddling or regulating, nor were they pleased with newly flourishing labor unions. In addition to causing crippling hunger and widespread unemployment, the Great Depression also inspired animosity for the wealthy and their incessant greed. There were mumblings about communism, workers rights, and cutting out middlemen. A revolution was brewing. To combat this, America's wealthiest desired to change the narrative. They knew the best way was to infuse everything they stood for with religion. So behind closed doors, they got crafty.

It wasn't long before Christian libertarianism was born. Funded by leaders of some of America's biggest corporations at the time, the message of Christian libertarianism was pushed in magazines, on the radio, and in the pulpit. Socialism and communism were demonized as anti-Christian and anti-American. General Motors, Chrysler, DuPont, and other corporations first pioneered this movement with the creation of the American Liberty League in 1934, but the league itself was dead by   77

1940. An anti-semitic preacher named James A. Fifield picked up the slack when he launched the organization Spiritual Mobilization as a way to end Christian support for welfare and to promote libertarianism. In California, Fifield preached to his wealthy congregation that "their riches were evidence of virtue rather than vice." The message that wealth was earned by blessings, not privilege or luck, was key to Christian libertarianism. Said writer and historian Kevin Kruse, "Both systems reflected a belief in the primacy of the individual: in Christianity, the saintly went to heaven and the sinners to hell, in capitalism, the worthy succeeded and the inept went broke." Under this cozy ideology, the rich could not be blamed for (or bothered with) the circumstances of the poor. Ever wondered why charities and publicized acts of philanthropy, as helpful as they can be, often intentionally do not address how capitalism chews up the poor? Spiritual Mobilization produced a lot of literature, and a well-liked mantra was "Freedom Under God." It was often uttered by Fifield, who once said that reading the bible was "like eating fish- we take the bones out to enjoy the meat. Not all parts of are equal value."

In radio programs and newsletters, greed was pitched as a fundamental Christian right, while biblical lessons about generosity and abstaining from greed, hypocrisy, or ostentatious displays of wealth... were downplayed or abandoned altogether. In a time that communist hating was at a fever pitch, excessive hard work and capitalism were championed as American ideals thanks to the mythification of the "hardworking Christian" identity. The composition of fiery religious passion and materialistic greed would later trickle to every race, but this initially exclusive prosperity gospel was a hit with white people... especially those who were desperate for a pa-

triotic and idealistic identity to cling to. But most cata-
lytic of the success of Christian libertarianism was that
the ideology coincided with the economic prosperity of
the post-World War II era. The American Dream seemed
more realistic than ever. To a generation raised during
the Great Depression, the opportunities for wealth
seemed endless for Americans who lived in the right
region of the country with the right skin color.

The most popular Christian libertarian preacher of the
mid-twentieth century was the Reverend Billy Graham,
who attracted to his flock both Texas oil tycoons and
poor farmers alike. His influence paved the way for
other "get rich through prayer, tithing, and hard work"
preachers who came after him, like Jim Bakker and
Creflo Dollar. Graham's influence was so great that in
1952 he convinced Congress to establish a national day
of prayer. He hadn't been the first to bring prayer to the
government, though. Ten years earlier Reverend Abraham Vereide successfully persuaded Congress to have
weekly prayer meetings. America was quietly becoming
a Christian nation; despite being established as a secular
one. But not just a Christian nation. A Christian nation
proud of greed, yet widely intolerant of things like racial
progression, cultural diversity, homosexuality, and
women's rights. Steadily, the fusion of American patriotism and Christianity by way of capitalism took hold
among anti-democrats (the same folks who evolved into
right-wing conservatives).Their influence, magnified by
the wealthy, had teeth. In 1954, "under God" was added
to the pledge of allegiance. In 1955, "In God We Trust"
was added to American money. It was accompanied by
an increased interest in returning to "wholesome American values", which not-so-mysteriously aligned with
white Christian ones.   79

Sex Work, Hard Work, and Selling Your Body For Money in the Land of Milk and Honey

We've all heard the old adage: if you can make it in New York, you can make it anywhere. We've also heard all the advice: don't move to New York if you have no money. While most of us broke entrepreneur/creative folks adhere to this sage wisdom and try our luck in America's other "it" cities, some of us can't resist the temptation of trying to become one of the big apple's success stories. You know, that one in a million creative that struck it big after they moved to New York with just a few months of rent paid, some bags, and a hunger for their brilliance to be recognized and prized. We go expecting endless opportunities, tropes from our favorite New York-based cinematic productions, and immediate mastery of the subway. Whether our understanding of New York comes from *Gossip Girl, Paid In Full, Law and Order, Sex and The City,* or *How To Make it In America*, we

KNOW it's expensive (as we've reiterated several times to concerned relatives), but we'll make it work. After all, that is the spirit of New York. It's the city where anything can happen with just the right bit of fortune or timing. We see people who were born and raised in the city thriving and underestimate everything that they've ever learned to survive. Not only do they know how to ride the subway, but they know how to rent spaces, how to save money, and how to make more of it in unexpected ways. There's a reason why New Yorkers have a reputation for being tough. The city will literally chew you up and spit you out alive. I learned this the hard way.

In the hazy aftermath of the civil war, northern laborers began grumbling about eight hour work days. During this industrial phase of capitalism, a "career" was a foreign concept to many Americans. Factory work was a torturous job endured by the masses. Roughly ⅓ of American laborers toiled away in factories for 14-16 hours per day in dangerous conditions for abysmal pay. There were strikes by Philadelphia workers in 1864 that called for 10 hour work days. The 8-hour concept became popular in Chicago that same year and workers won a vaguely worded and hardly enforced state law. But the first real change came about in New York. Adopting a movement previously smeared across Europe, National Labor Union backed workers in New York won the treat of eight hour work days in 1872.

Suck on that for a moment. 145 years ago, when most states did not recognize black people as citizens and a handful of names like Rockefeller and Astor lorded over everyone, eight hour work days were set as the standard for humane working conditions. In the decades that followed, more conditions were put in place to   81 protect the American worker... but not nearly enough to compare to the ones put in place to benefit the super wealthy.

In the same city where eight hour work days were first guaranteed on American soil, the cost of living for average folks has soared well beyond forty hour work weeks. Unless you're an investment banker, lawyer, celebrity, start-up guru, or something of that nature. But for the city's millions of retail, fast food, and service workers, living in New York is painfully stressful. Rent, transportation, food, and utilities add up. Then there is the stress that wreaks havoc on your psyche, like tiny living quarters, roommates, frequently late trains, and the infamous mid-day dead phone battery. Of course, this is where people chime in and claim that these people could work elsewhere if they want money to live comfortably. But if nobody works the retail, fast food, and service jobs, who would the rich people yell at or order around?

If you're like the average person obsessed with New York, your first vacation to the city is magnificent. The food. The beautiful buildings and people. The noise and rush of a bustling mecca. You even feel cool when you ride the subway. I know I did. I have always loved the city since a family trip at the age of 12, but a carefully planned return visit during my college sophomore summer reignited my passion. After that weekend I returned back to Ohio and made a plan to move to the city the following summer. I began saving as much as I could from my freelancing and blog earnings and got a job at Ohio State's 24-hour library as a third shift security associate. The entire year all I could think about was New York. It certainly helped that my boyfriend at the time lived there, and I visited him nearly once a month. Each trip was like my first vacation: it was over before it had started, and 'd leave the city on a bus foaming with anger that I was headed back to Ohio. The months flicked by, and in April I began searching for an apartment. My boyfriend was away at trucking school, and in a rush of excitement, I foolishly reserved a 7x12 bedroom "nook" in someone's upper east side apartment for three months without even seeing it in person first. The apartment was paid three months in full and I arrived with $1000. My hopes were high that I could move there, find part-time work, and supplement my income by dog-walking. In my free time, I hoped to soak up the city's nightlife, network my ass off, and continue my career as an entertainment blogger.

At the end of that hellacious Summer I was crawling back to Ohio for my senior year, destitute and deflated although not completely defeated. The city had violated me in every way, and I had barely survived thanks to weekly deposits from my boyfriend and one consistent dog walking client. The one good thing that happened to me that summer was an epiphany after a penthouse party with internet celebrities in Brooklyn. Like many college seniors faced with the threat of post-graduate life, I had been bewildered up until that point about what my career was going to be. After that party all I knew was that I wanted to write and teach about history and get paid well for it so I could give back to the community. I no longer wanted to do celebrity blogging. "My life goals are to educate the brainwashed and make hella money so I can send it to the community." I tweeted on August 8th, 2015. While my career goals changed, my dream city did not. I vowed to return to New York when I graduated and tough it out. I knew that I

83

needed to return with a sufficient amount of money or I would once more be pushed from the city. So I worked harder and saved more, doing the 32 maximum hours allowed at the library nearly every week.

But around January, I realized that my New York fund was not where it needed to be. I began freaking out. I was set to graduate in August, and that was the same month that my lease expired. For all four years my college and living expenses had been handled, and real adulthood loomed around the corner. I know I didn't want to return to my high school self either, a girl with no social life who had three jobs. Back in those days both sleep and my social life were virtually nonexistent. So with August rapidly approaching and my savings barely growing, I decided to take the plunge into sex work. Here's an unpublished column (with a few personal details altered) that I wrote at the time.

> *If you would have asked me just two months ago would I ever be a cam girl, you would have gotten laughed at. A horrible, shrieking laugh that would make the back of your neck tingle. Two months ago camming was on the same list as porn, teaching, and employment at Chick Fil A: things I had once considered but had ultimately decided against. I love my body, I gave up the battle against being called a hoe long ago, and I regularly post thirst traps... but to become a cam girl seemed like something incredibly cliché. Exploitation, burning out, daddy issues, yadda yadda. Then abruptly during my senior year of college, I got tired of being broke. I got tired of jostling funds from my dwindling savings account so I could pay my light bill and purchase coconut oil and bags of frozen vegetables. The meager earnings*

from my work study job would never bankroll my upcoming post-grad plans to move to New York let alone help me pay off my current bill of debt or enjoy a slightly better quality of life. I thought about selling weed but my paranoia only allows me to smoke, not commit felonies. And so I wrestled with these two alternatives for months: continue being broke or start selling weed. A few times I reminded myself that I could get a second or completely new job, but listening to friends complain about their shitty employment avenues repulsed me. Don't get me wrong, I applied for several jobs but I wasn't exactly sad that I wasn't deemed suitable for any of the positions. Chasing after barely above minimum wage earnings and khaki pants dress codes did not appeal to me. My friends were beckoning me over to their personal hells and I didn't want any parts. Graduates on the east coast in sales, making pennies on the dollar for asshole bosses, but thankful they found a damned job. Writer friends in New York pulling double shifts in retail barely making enough for rent and supplementing their grocery budget by writing for fledgling blogs. Friends working at call centers making decent money to surrender their nights and weekends and free time, doing redundant work that only fuels their need to drink or smoke regularly for stimulation. In the background were my stripper pals, pulling in thousands a week. They were purchasing cars, moving away from home, and paying the health bills of various family members. I envied them and their money, but the thought of letting anyone touch me with rough and ashy hands stopped me from crossing that line. Then the universe, as if tired of seeing me be a broke bitch who stole lipstick and tampons   85 *from CVS, intervened. I watched a girl on twitter periscope while on cam. She rolled a blunt, shook her ass, and played on her phone for 30 minutes and made about $100. I signed up on cam about an hour later. Two days later I was given the green light and my life changed forever. I was (and still am) despondent to any notion that everyone in my personal, social, and professional circles will find out that I play with my privates for money online. I have a general idea of how the big wigs would respond: claims of disappointment and tears that would be incomparable to my personal disgust at my pre-cam bank account balance. I'm expected to not ask for help, but I don't find brownie points in the struggle. I don't find joy in incessant amounts of labor. Is that a crime? I've been struggling and working all my life, thanks.... And I want to live nice. Getting myself off from the privacy of my own home for guys all across the world didn't register to me as much as making tons of money did. In my first week of camming, I was on my period, I didn't masturbate, I didn't show my vagina, I had no idea what I was doing, and I only worked 14 hours. In that one week, I made $2000.... An amount that would take me 248 hours to achieve at my day job. Hello. Do you even have to ask? I'm a cam girl now. Do you know how hard it is to go to a job where you make eight dollars an hour when you just made $500 to play with your vibrator for an hour? Extremely.*

There are some feminists who believe there is no such thing as consensual sex work due to economic coercion. I don't fully agree. Some women enjoy sex work and take pride in it the same way others take pride in their own conventional jobs. Some women, like a dear friend of mine with two degrees and wealthy parents, strip because the income and flexible hours allows her to pursue her passions in a way that a more traditional career would not allow. She enjoys stripping and sporadically finds it annoying the same way another friend of mine love-hates her waitressing job at an upscale restaurant. However, I do admit that the overwhelming majority of women (and people in general) involved in consensual sex work have resorted to the career because they were not making enough money to sustain a basic quality of life. I was not one of these women. I chose sex work because I wanted to upgrade my lifestyle and begin building my dreams without dedicating forty hour weeks of my life to someone else's business. I did what some like to say is "taking the easy way out."

My journey into consensual sex work is not meant to invoke pity, nor am I trying to encourage anyone into it. My experiences were mine alone, and they were positive. I learned a few new sexual preferences, got tons of studying done on cam, and had more money than I ever had in my life. I also got to pay off a few debts and be generous with my money. A few of my friends were shocked that I began offering to pay for drinks or fork over gas money. Camming was life changing.

With the money I made from camming, I successfully created a nest egg for moving to New York that made my second experience start off much more enjoyable and worthwhile. My foundation was made more solid by my securement of a full-time job at Equinox Gym, where I would make about $1400 a month after taxes. With three months rent paid in advance, I believed I could focus on writing my first book and putting my degree to use in my own way. However, by the fourth month, 87 the forty hour work weeks were beginning to interfere with my creativity. A falling out with my con-artist landlord rendered me nearly homeless just three months after I moved to the city. My wallet begged me to return to cam work, but the increased popularity of the camming website I once used meant there was a higher chance that I'd be spotted by friends, family, or one of the thousands of new followers I gained on 9/11. I wasn't ashamed, but I didn't want my credibility as an intellectual to be ruined.

To increase my income I had begun babysitting my boss's child, but it wasn't very lucrative. The popularity of my twitter meant more opportunities than before and there simply wasn't any time to get things done when I was constantly at work. So I followed the advice of my followers to raise money for my own media company on GoFundMe, quit my job, and moved across the country so I could focus on beginning Intelexual Media. I cannot express how privileged I am to have recieved that initial $10,000 start-up from my social media supporters. It allowed me to hire a graphic designer, print my first book, buy filming equipment, and establish myself as a virtual educator. Though in total transparency, virtual educating isn't as lucrative as other "internet famous" careers, especially because I'm hellbent on providing most of my content for free and most people don't like paying for information that makes them uncomfortable. Even still, I truck on because educating is my passion. In the present day, I still sometimes engage in sex work as a virtual dominatrix or foot fetish model when my budget is a little too tight. I have been fortunate to have endless support from people who refuse to let my status as a sex worker define me. They understand that it doesn't negate my intelligence or zeal for educating.

The third installment of my column about camming was titled *Is Your Job as Exploitative As Mine? (Probably)*. While I never wrote it, I want to expand on the title here. For starters, let me freely admit that cam work is not fully comparable to escorting or stripping, both of which require physical contact with a paying client. Even still, while arguments rage in snooty pro-sex feminist circles about a totem pole of sex work, I believe it's all the same. Whether you engage in consensual fetish modeling, porn, escorting, stripping, camming, phone sex, dominatrixing, or anything in between, you are exchanging sexual arousal and/or gratification for money. Sex work is sex work. But to too many Americans, sex work isn't thought of as work at all. In fact, it's often used as a reason to invalidate someone's accomplishments. Only recently have American sex workers (and the women who are an eviction notice away from becoming one of them) demanded to be taken seriously in their other career pursuits. In the not so distant past, one's sexual life, or even something as trivial as a nude picture, had the power to end a career. Even though it is a new era where former strippers and escorts can move into anything from fashion design to rapping, the stigma s still there.

Let's stand at a crossroads between two points. At point A, you are told to hustle by any means necessary. If eight hour work days do not bring the income you desire, work harder and longer. Get creative or become a step on someone else's road to success because America rewards hustlers. But the stats about social mobility and wealth disparity say otherwise. Today, the richest 1% of families own 36% of the nation's wealth, which is twice as much as the bottom 90% owns. The slice of pie that belongs to the top 1% has been growing since the 89

20th century and shows no sign of slowing down. 30% of the workforce earns near minimum wage. That's 21 million people. Less than half of them are between 16 and 24. These jobs are largely in retail and food industries, where innovation in automation and online shopping threaten job security. Not that these jobs are actually worth having. Many experts agree that minimum wage jobs, even when worked for forty hours per week, do not cover the average cost of living in ANY American state. At a severe disadvantage are black Americans, whose wealth does not match that of whites. Thirty years ago the median black family had wealth of $6800. Today it is $1700, compared to the median white household wealth of $116,000. In case you're wondering, thirty years ago the median white family wealth was $102,000. If black wealth continues to decrease at the same rate, it will be near zero by the year 2053. For shits and giggles, I'll throw in the fact that it costs at least $245,000 (not including self-care, emergency medical fees, or fancy bells and whistles) to raise a single child to the age of 18. Now factor in dwindling health care coverage and soaring costs of college and housing. It is cognitive dissonance that makes people ignore stats like these and despise sex workers more than the system that coerced most into the life.

At point B, you are told that consensual sex work is exploitative and "selling your body". Funnily enough, damaging one's body through strenuous work like coal mining and professional athletics do not warrant the same observations. Even if the NFL ever acknowledges the dangers of CTE or addresses the significant damage a life of contact sports brings, you'll never hear players being chastised for selling or damaging their body for money. Some will say it's because what they do takes talent.

Other critics will say it's because they are doing hard work as if consensual sex work is easy. This is untrue. It's like in any other job where labor is required so that you can pay your bills (even when you're tired, stressed, or sick). Sex work can involve mental gymnastics, creativity, problem-solving, fatigue, research, fitness, styling, dance routines, and exhausting conversations with people who bore you to tears. Despite all of the work put in by sex workers, a lot of underpaid and exploited laborers look down on them as lazy and immoral. "She had other options," people love to say from their pedestals when judging sex workers. Even if they themselves are struggling to survive with their conventional jobs, they regard sex workers with contempt for not taking the noble and hardworking way like them. It's pathetic. But then again, our ideas about hard work and sex work have been molded by propaganda and misogyny.

We champion hard work even though the country's wealthiest people are often born with money. Hard work is supposed to bring you the gratification of a job well done and money is just the bonus. The popular marketing concepts of "never sleeping" and "no days off", encourage most average working class people to labor themselves silly so they can fatten the pockets of chuckling executives. Money backed by "hard work" (aka exploitation) is more respected than money made by sex work. Being able to brag about a rags to riches story (without resorting to "selling yourself") is the desire for many people who erroneously think they can save their measly paychecks into the upper echelon. Don't believe me? Go through the comment section on any of Cardi B's pictures on Instagram and you'll see someone angrily declaring something along the lines of "I never had to sell my body and I live the good life! If I can do it, we   91 all can." It's a real kick watching exploited people create ways for themselves to feel superior to others.

In addition to deep-rooted and nonsecular views on sexuality, it is misogyny that causes vehement opposition to the rights and protection of sex workers. Some of the same people who applaud Jay Z for moving from drug dealer to legit billionaire will malign former sex workers trying to do the same thing. Similarly, descendants of dirty slaves and imperialism empires (the roots of the wealth imbalance in this country) somehow consider their money cleaner than that of sex workers. But how can we continue to ignore the reasons why sex work is so common? A lot of people enjoy trading money for sexual release. This has remained true since the dawn of time. With a constant stream of eager clientele, sex work continues to be lucrative even if people don't actually like sex workers. It may not be easy money, but it is reliable money.... which is a draw for people struggling to make ends meet.

In a country with skyrocketing costs of living, mounting college debt, and decreasing well paying blue collar jobs, it is no wonder at all that more and more people find themselves in sex work. When you examine racial, gender, and class intersections- you'll notice it's particularly prevalent among women of color and trans people. This arouses two dichotomous concerns. One, sex workers are often the target of violence because of the stigma attached to them. Two, it is in sex work that the two groups of people most often marginalized and underpaid can achieve financial stability with little start-up costs or skills necessary. This is economic coercion. When the bills are due and emergencies happen, sex work is there. When a person has no skills or employment opportunities and needs to escape dangerous situations, sex work is there. When the 40 hour work weeks at a monotonous multi-million dollar company begin taking a toll (and the heavily taxed checks barely leave room in your budget for a savings account, let alone self-care) sex work is there. This has been the bittersweet comfort for me and millions of other women throughout the centuries who have, at one point in time, anticipated economic hardship. Sex work, hard work. It's all the same.

Black Bodies [Fear, Fascination, and Fetishization]

The bodies of black people have long enthralled the masses, from initial contact with Europeans to modern times where imitation has evolved into an annoying and obnoxious gesture of flattery. We live in an interesting time period of plastic surgery, ass injections, and expensive creams that promise to 'stimulate' fat cells. This is a time where a certain celebrity woman had no butt in 2007 and now has the mother of all asses in 2017- and coyly denies having any work done (and people believe her)! This is a time where 'big black cock' and 'interracial cuckold' are highly popular porn categories. Big body parts are a big deal. But that hasn't always been the case. Historically, the black body has been subject to ridicule, speculation, and outright cruelty. Up until the 21st century, big body parts -often exaggerated and caricatured in depictions of black people- have been associated with lewdness, incivility, and inferiority. These ideas took hold before the inception of slavery, and survived for centuries after its demise.

Time has withered former thoughts about big black body parts, and now they are some of the most coveted and imitated in the world. So much so that we live in an era where some black women who don't fit conventional body expectations- big butts, hips, and lips- admit to feeling less authentically black. This feeling of inadequacy extends to black men, who sometimes feel like monster sized dicks are a requirement of a valid black male identity. How did we arrive here? Why have black bodies served as a backdrop to racism and cruelty since the first European laid eyes on them in the 15th century? Before we delve into the twisted history of the black body and the white people who obsessed over them, let me tell you about a guy we'll call Sir Peanut Butter.

He was a fine black man with a gorgeous body and a tiny micropenis. I was just a high schooler when he sent me a picture of what appeared to be his gigantic dick in a pair of boxers. What happened next remains one of the strangest moments in my life. We agreed to meet for a hook up. He rejected my offer for head and instead delivered amazing cunnilingus. He bent me over the arm of the couch we were nestled on. I urged him to put on a condom, and he did. As soon as he slid into me, everything felt strange. His dick felt entirely too stiff. I then felt something cool on my butt cheek as he penetrated me deeper. I turned around. His boxers were still on. Over the boxers was a harnessed dildo with silver rings on the straps wrapped around his thighs. I laughed at him and cried out in anger, calling him a fraud and throwing things at him because I felt betrayed. Looking back, how I handled that situtation with Sir Peanut Butter is one of my biggest regrets. When he informed me that he had a micropenis, I did not stop to understand or empathize. I got mad at him for not having a big dick.

I wish I could give you the exact words I typed out on my cracked iPhone 4s screen during my sophomore year of college when I rehashed this story to a small yet enthusiastic percentage of black twitter, but this was before threads and I couldn't locate all the tweets. My mentions did not slow down for days on end, as men and women alike dropped by to add more jokes or simply add a 'lmao'. Out of thousands of mentions, only two or three people criticized me for the story. Looking back on this story that inflated my followers in a fortnight, I cringe for a number of reasons. First of all, I told the story without any empathy for the man involved. He had no more control over the size of his penis than I did. I did and still do feel betrayed that he tried to trick me, but age has allowed me to ask a few questions that I hadn't considered at the time.

Why did Mr. Peanut Butter feel the need to lie about his size? Why did I seek a big dick, and become so disappointed when I saw that he didn't have one? Why did I feminize him because of his micro-penis? Why did people who read my story laugh at him, not realizing that he had no control over the size of his penis? Lastly, would I really have still accepted him and his tiny penis if he hadn't of tried to trick me? After mulling over these questions, I wondered about how similar black men with small penises are to black women who lack hips and booty. They feel left out, targeted, or ridiculed. How and why do we consciously and subconsciously devalue peoples' blackness because they don't fit our expectations of what the black body is?

The lore surrounding Africans before mass European arrival to the continent was shrouded in mystery; with tales of cannibalism, untold wealth, and extremely horny savages who inhabited the land. In 1526 a Spanish Moroccan Moor named Leo Africanus influenced a popular thought about Africa by declaring that "There is no nation under heaven more prone to venery." To outsiders, the continent was awash with horny natives. There was no distinguishing between the thousands of cultures that existed, either- they were all sexual beasts. The ebony shellacked bodies of African men rippled with muscles borne of frequent hunting and physical labor. The cherry on top were there allegedly big penises; so awe-inducing that for a short period of time it became en vogue among European scientists and explorers to own one. "...that the penis of an African is larger than that of an European... has been shown in every anatomical school in London. Preparations of them are preserved in most anatomical museums, and I have one in mine." wrote English surgeon Charles White in 1799. Years later, American scientist Andrew Tyfe instructed students to find large penises for dissection. Shapely black women with all sizes of breasts, hips, and rotund booties made white men have strange feelings about the savages that they never expected to have. The European response to these majestic and strange bodies was fascination, fear, and ignorance so deep that it would serve as a harsh backdrop to race relations for over four centuries and counting.

For some reason, initial Europeans who made contact with Africa were convinced that the inhabitants were either direct descendants of monkeys or engaged in sexual behavior with them. Yes, you read that right. European explorers thought indigenous peoples in Africa were having sex with primates. "Disingenuous and unmanly position hath been formed, and privately handed to again, which is this, that the negros, though in their figure carry some resemblance of manhood, yet are indeed no man." claimed one explorer, who clearly believed that the two groups copulated. The line between primate and Africans was so blurred that characteristics between the two groups were projected onto each other by experts of the day. Primates were noted during those times as extremely hypersexual, so it is no surprise that explorers would come to apply the trademark to Africans. As explorer Edward Topsell put it, "Men that have low and flat nostrils are libidinous as apes that attempt women, and having thick lipides the upper hanging over the neather, they are deemed fools like the lips of asses and apes."

The perceived highly sexual nature of Africans wasn't just limited to the men, either. When describing African women, one explorer commented they had a "temper hot and lascivious, making no scruple to prostitute themselves to the Europeans for a very slender profit, so great is their inclination to white men." White men arrived, and ego stemming from their false sense of superiority and ownership created ignorant monsters. Both black men and women were enveloped into the category of hypersexual as if European countries weren't teeming with brothels and syphilis.

In some African cultures, prostitution was a religious ritual. In a Zimbabwe temple, kings daughters were offered as sacred 'prostitutes'. Among the Lele people, communal wives for unmarried men were considered one of the highest ranked villagers. Tribal dancing and reports of polygamy only added fire to the flame of sexual deviance, but the black body itself really intensified the beliefs of explorers. Due to Africa's climate, indigenous people smartly wore little to no clothing. Despite the fact that nudity was normal and necessary, and not a gesture of sexual deviance, European explorers linked their lack of clothing to the nakedness of animals- in particular, the primate. Though ludicrous to most in contemporary times, explorers believed primates and Africans (both things they had never seen before) looked alike.

The presumed hypersexuality of black men continued to be amplified by their larger than average penises, a reputation that would carry through to slavery. In 1781 a William Feltman remarked, "I can assure you it would surprise a person to see these [damned] black boys how well they are hung." The appendages of black male bodies fascinated scholars of the day, and soon the idea of black male sexual superiority took hold. As historian Winthrop D. Jordan put it, "By the final quarter of the 18th century the idea that the negroes penis was larger than the white mans' had become something of a commonplace in European scientific circles." Jealousy was sure to follow. Even the richest of white men couldn't buy a new penis, and any sense of superiority was soured by this fact. This alleged sexual inferiority would cause a deep fear in white men that manifested itself in cruelty. Even if they thought themselves sexually inferior, whites could rest easy knowing they stamped out the masculinity of black men in other ways.

While the black male body inspired fear, the black

female body inspired fascination. The curvy bodies of African women scantily clad in weather appropriate clothing intrigued white men and aroused their sexual interest. To Europeans, African women were the very antithesis of white women- dark, uncivilized, and not virtuous. It is my guess that white men were disgusted with themselves for being sexually attracted to the complete opposite of their own women. This disgust developed into the excuse that African women were seductresses with an insatiable lust for white men.

Perhaps the most famous example of the public exploitation of black women is the story of Sarah Baartman, also known as the Hottentot Venus. Sarah was born in the late 1780's to the Khoisan group of indigenous people near what is now South Africa. She was a tall woman with a huge butt, characteristic of Khoisan women. She had two children who died young, and once dated a drummer in the Dutch infantry named Hendrick Van Jong. While working as a wet nurse in Capetown, a Scottish surgeon named William Dunlop (who also brought animal specimens from Africa to Europe on the side) convinced Sarah to move to England and exhibit her body. Hendrick Caesars, a free black, was her boss at the time and he agreed to go with her. Sarah was allegedly provided with a contract where she would share in the profits, but just five years after her European debut she died without a penny to her name. With her pretty feet, rumored-to-be long labia lips, and massively protruding buttocks, she captivated England, where patrons could come see her for two shillings a pop. This price included watching her walk around solemnly and silently with face paint and feathers, puffing on a pipe in a tight body stocking.

Though Sarah rarely spoke in front of crowds, she did speak Dutch, some English, and learned a little bit of French. Baartman appeared to be nude in her shows, but it was actually the tight flesh-colored bodysuit that gave this illusion. She refused to expose her vagina, even when offered money. However for a few extra coins, one could touch the Hottentot Venus, though she didn't exactly respond too well to this. Described one patron, "One pinched her; one gentleman poked her with his cane; one lady employed her parasol to ascertain that all was, as she called it, 'nattral.' This inhuman baiting the poor creature bore with sullen indifference, except upon some provocation, when she seemed inclined to resent brutality.... On these occasions, it took all the authority of the keeper to subdue her resentment."

The African Association, an abolitionist society, championed for Baartman's release. As the abolitionist movement began to grow popular in London, people questioned the ethics of parading around a nude-ish African woman. It is highly contested among historians whether or not Baartman had any say in her own affairs, but evidence points to both summations. Baartman owned the copyright to her first two press images, but she died broke without family, friends, or management just five years after her European debut. She claimed to be free during a hearing initiated by The African Association, but her testimony could have been swayed by the men who brought her to Europe. The hearing made her a European sensation and Sarah was soon in high demand. Baartman and her managers traveled around Europe before settling in Paris, where she performed for 18 months. By June of 1815, Baartman had been "sold" to an animal trainer, and there is evidence she began performing at brothels, and even speculation that she 101 began prostituting to support herself. By December 1815 she was dead. When Sarah died, her body was quickly acquired by George Cuvier, Napolean Bonaparte's surgeon general. After casting a mold of her body, dissecting her genitalia, and comparing her private parts to primates, there was now erroneous scientific proof that black people were inferior and animalistic in nature. Her occupation as a semi-nude freak show performer only bolstered Cuvier's argument that Africans were not only lesser human beings, but hypersexual ones as well.

To Europeans, Baartman's butt was as freaky and disturbing as conjoined twins, little people, or people with missing limbs. In fact, she was billed as "The Greatest Phenomenon Ever Exhibited In [France]." Though it sounded like an honor, it was very much an insult. She was awe-inspiring, but only because she was advertised as grotesque and only appealing to Africans. White men who went to see her did not admit to sexual arousal or interest, just curiosity at an African freak. European satirists were not fooled by those who feigned disgust by her shapely figure, however. The 1814 play *The Hottentot Venus, or Hatred of French Women* criticized those who flocked to see Baartman, accusing them of preferring savages to civilized French women. The plot involved a classy woman named Amelia trying to save her cousin from the clutches of a "savage Hottentot". Because it was heavily implied that no white man in his right mind would ever find African women attractive, the evil black seductress stereotype was strengthened.

Baartman's story illustrates how the hypersexual reputation of black women functioned. Her body was exotic to Europeans, but also repulsive. Her willingness to display it according to her cultural norms (modesty to her meant keeping her vagina covered with a loincloth, both intrigued Europeans and encouraged negative thoughts about all African women. The nudity of Baartman and other African women was twisted into an assumption that they were sexually insatiable. In Europe, only whores exposed copious amounts of skin which meant the invaders of African land conflated the scantily clad black women with European prostitutes. When carted off to trading posts after their transatlantic journey, the soon to be slaves were almost always presented naked, where potential buyers appraised their bodies for labor and childrearing value. The entire experience was embarrassing for the slave and could be sexually charged. One observer of the trading post noted: "If negresses are put up, scandalous and indecent questions and jests are permitted." It was a mortifying and degrading event in the lives of each bonded man or woman who experienced it, particularly for those who made the transatlantic journey from free human to chattel slave.

Black bodies were synonymous with currency for white men, and black sex was even more valuable because it could result in more property. They were not people with valid thoughts or feelings- they were machines. Output labor and babies, perform more labor and have more babies ... repeat. Their ability to produce children was prized. Because the spirit of masculinity was extinguished by the bonds of slavery, the penises of male slaves- and ultimately sex- became their only instruments of power and status. Perhaps a male slave could not own property or stop Massa from raping his wife, but he had some sense of ownership over his dick. Virility was attributed to black men. It was their arena. Sex was something he didn't need permission, status, or the correct skin color to have.

103

So back to Sir Peanut Butter. In many cultures, penis size serves as a symbol of manhood. But for black men especially, who have been historically disenfranchised at every turn, savoring the white man's jealousy of their sexual reputation is routine. But what about the men who don't have large beef sticks? They live their lives with the daunting knowledge that women of all races expect them to fulfill a size quota. Mr. Peanut Butter's micropenis made him feel like less of a man. His skin color made this self-realization much harsher, as he knew that women like me expected him to have a dick close in size to a salami. When he faked having a large penis, it was less about impressing me and more about fulfilling an aspiration he had for himself. All the black pornos I have ever seen involve men with gargantuan cocks, and that ideal gripped my desires- so I'm pretty sure it influenced his too. The "black men have bigger dicks" stereotype may hold scientific merit, but it also creates a problematic expectation that a lot of our men feel that they need to adhere to.

The same can be said for many black women who aren't thick. Hip-hop culture glorifies big butts, and a quick twitter search will tell you that some skinny black women often feel neglected or devalued. Kim Kardashian and her ass plumping sisters aren't the only ones paying for figures reminiscent of the Hottentot Venus. Celebrities like Nicki Minaj and Blac Chyna are proof that black women are also trying to achieve an ideal of black womanhood that has pervaded since before slavery. Having a big butt or a big dick has unfortunately come to be seen as vital components of black womanhood and manhood, respectively.

When Europeans arrived in Africa they placed black people into two categories that would succeed as debilitating stereotypes in the centuries that followed. Black men were highly sexual studs who only acted right when under the control of slavery. Black women were insatiable harlots. Both of these speculations were based on the black bodies themselves. It was easy to make these ideas popular through art and household products that regularly depcted highly sexualized black bodies. With this propaganda, both black men and women were whittled into sexual predators incapable of being victims or sexually autonomous beings. The excuse of blacks as lecherous sinners meant that white men and women had a ready-made defense for any exposure of nterracial sexual activity- it was the negro's fault, not theirs.

"I Don't Treat Whores Like Human Beings" [Understanding the History and Culture That Puts Black Girls at risk]

Disclaimer: I found "Sex Worker" to be too broad of a term for this essay. The language used is colorful, not inflammatory.

I don't treat whores like human beings. It was my sophomore year of college when I read those words in a tweet from a guy who, much later, I found out tried to rape a good friend of mine. He was one of those guys who liked to talk about body counts and instagram hoe attire. He regularly denounced black women as "dick hungry whores", and I had been added to that list after denying his sexual advances during my freshman year. I no longer followed him by the time I saw that tweet, but when I did it made me ill. He was moderately attractive, so he had a gaggle of women who retweeted his misogynistic tweets for validation and cool points. This time it was actually a male acquaintance who retweeted his foul words. I blocked the both of them right then and there, but that sentence has remained etched in my brain ever since I first read it. *I don't treat whores like human beings.* He was scum as it is, but I think about all of our mutual associates who have kicked it with him since he typed those words. I think of all of our common pals who continued to follow him and recently retweeted pictures of him in a moist Ohio club with a dog leash connected to some silly girl's neck. I only bring him up because the same people who retweet and interact with him also tweeted about the recent wave of missing girls in the DC area.

As we all know, slavery was rife with the sexual exploitation of black women. It occurred for centuries with little interference or aid for the victims, as slave women were considered property with no rights. Sexual assault on a slave was not a crime. Actually, miscegenation was almost always pinned on the black person involved. Black women were wanton and insatiable jezebels capable of seducing even the most honorable of white men into their beds. Their identity was the complete antithesis of the pure and modest white woman, whose virtue was to be protected at all costs. To be completely clear, white women were not immune to sexual abuse, but their whiteness came stamped with virtue and some value of victimhood. Assaulting a white woman, especially if you were black, was reprehensible. As reported by the equal justice initiative, nearly one in four black people lynched from 1877 to 1945 were accused of improper contact with a white woman.

There was no such lynching epidemic in response to the frequent sexual assaults of black women. There was no opportunity for them to be victims because they were torpedoed by white society as sexually insatiable predators. It was a perfect excuse for antebellum era white rapists to have their way with black women. "Plenty of the colored women have children by the white men. She know better than to not do what he say," recalled one former slave in 1937. Black women were for the taking because nobody cared about their abuse. This sentiment was echoed after slavery during the violent years of reconstruction and the Jim Crow south.

The Jezebel stereotype isn't the only reason sexual exploitation has historically been so prevalent among black women. Through the years they did not have the social, political, or economic power to complain. In addition to the obvious violent rapes we think about, black women faced a much more sneaky kind of sexual coercion. Thanks to their carefully carved status as second-class citizens, black women were often desperate for employment and money. For starters, they earned less than their white and male counterparts... which was only exacerbated by the commonality of single-parent households. The desperation and helplessness of these women was preyed upon.

When John Griffith secretly toured the south as a black man in *Black Like Me*, he encountered a particularly nasty man in Alabama who talked about how "all of the white men in the region craved colored girls." He went on to explain the hiring requirement for his black female employees. "I've had it in every one of them before they ever got on the payroll... if they want to eat... or feed their kids. If they don't put out, they don't get the job." Again, desperation is a nasty reality because it keeps victims quiet. "Alabama nigger women are good about that. They won't ever go to the cops or tell on you," he added.

Let's state the obvious. The relative ease of committing an act of prostitution means many bills would have never been paid and many families would have gone unsupported without black and brown legs being spread. I'm not just talking about career hookers who were pushed into the life by pimps or abuse during their early years; void of proper educations or support systems to keep them afloat. Nor am I just talking about the women born from the brisk sexual unions of various scarlet women and their johns; involved in the life from childhood. I'm also talking about the black women who screwed their scamming landlords for a rent extension or blew a crooked cop to get the family breadwinner out of the backseat of the squad car. One can't help but to think of the endless amounts of women who have ever been forced to sell pussy to make ends meet or simply survive the realities of poverty. Not every black woman walked down these paths, but more than enough have. Too many have been exploited both in plain sight and behind the scenes, creating a societal numbness to sexual exploitation.

A field of factors have historically led women of all races into prostitution, but racially charged poverty made black women prime candidates for the career path during the 20th century. It's because of American capitalism, wrapped in greasy wax paper with a batch of wealth disparity piled high on the side and an ice cold cup of racism to wash it all down. Women of any race, including the black one, should not be economically 109 coerced into prostitution for survival... but they are. An even more unfortunate reality? A large portion of these women happen to be of color. It's irreverent proof of the greed of American capitalism and a very important byproduct of our racial history that too many people look past when justifying the exploitation of our women. There is no justification for a country that pushes women into sex work for basic quality of life, though soulless humans do manage to scrape up crappy excuses involving accusations of immorality and laziness. But what about the immorality and laziness of the cops and the justice system? Why do prostitution laws seem to largely punish the girls and women involved more than the men? It's a conversation that receives little play from prominent black voices.

Now how does everything I just said tie into the epidemic of missing black girls and women?

The mainstream media doesn't care too much about missing black girls or their sexual abuse. When black girls go missing they are usually categorized as runaways, if they are even reported on. A lot of people don't even think runaways are worth looking for. They don't think about what the girls are running from; instead theorizing that they're probably off being "fast" with a boyfriend. They don't think about the people these girls can run into, who know nobody is really looking for them. They don't think about the breaking in. The gang rapes. The degradation. The beatings. The dehumanization.

Most of us have only heard about these girls on social media, making it feel like nothing is being done. Adding to the sense of helplessness is the very unfortunate truth that not enough black people think about sexually exploited women or how they came to be.

When I see tweets on the timeline of people asking about the recently publicized disappearances of DMV area girls, its bittersweet. Sweet because people are paying attention but bitter because this is a bigger beast than people are comprehending. For every girl found, another girl goes missing. Human trafficking has been thriving under the radar long before the recent news of 64,000 missing black girls and women surfaced. Furthermore, black girls have been the prime targets of pimps and sex trafficking for decades now. In fact, 40% of sex trafficking victims are estimated to be black, a disproportionately high number when considering we only make up 13% of the population. It is a problem that can only be fixed by radical change, not retweets and relying on police. The first wave of radical change comes about by attacking attitudes and harmful ideologies that put our girls at risk. It begins with making people aware of how we perpetuate the system of sexual exploitation.

At the very top of the list is capitalism, which is an entire beast of its own. But on a simpler level, our attitudes contribute to the apathy of black human trafficking victims. Most people have a hard time connecting kidnapped girls and runaway victims with career prostitutes. For most people, if there is any empathy for a young runaway or kidnapping victim, it is gone by the time she is broken and fully immersed in the life. She "could get out if she wanted," as a former acquaintance would put it, ignoring the harsh realities of intense mental and sexual abuse that create some lifelong sex workers. But I saw that same acquaintance tweet his dismay about those missing girls in DC. He, like most 111 people, doesn't think about the fact that most of these girls grow up to become the women that he and too few others care about. They think about hoes versus women, good girls versus fast girls. They care about the women and the good girls while blaming the fast girls and hoes for their misfortune.

The gag? You can't care about one group and not the other. These groups are two components of one fluid cycle. A cycle built on the fast girl vs good girl ideologies and hoe versus housewives mentalities. The kind of cycle that loves to say troubled young girls who attract the attention of grown men are asking for whatever bad things might happen to them. A cycle strengthened by a society that encourages poor self-esteem and body shame in young girls. Per a forensic psychologist to CNN on sex trafficking victims, "What is similar to some of those girls that I work with is their self-esteem or lack thereof. You either become vulnerable to a man on the street or a man you meet in school. You become vulnerable because you're looking for attention."

This is a cycle catalyzed by devaluing girls who don't have fathers and women who don't have men. You know, putting relationship and familial love over self-love. Shoutout to the fatherless jokes and "you're bitter because you're single" roasts. This is a cycle well oiled by the people who dismiss R Kelly's sexual abuse of black teen girls because they "wanted to get peed on." You know, it was okay for a grown man to forget the law and any semblance of human decency because his teenage victims "wanted his attention and they got it." Most of all it is a cycle that relies on society's apathy for whores. There will always be men like the asshat who tweeted that he doesn't treat whores like human beings. But the power we choose to give these men is what makes them so dangerous. People still followed that sexual predator after his endless tweets of misogyny. People assumed he was joking or even worse, they simply didn't care. They approved an attitude that is permissive of violating whores and sluts, freaks and jezebels. Their reasoning? "Don't be a hoe if you don't want to be treated like one." With attitudes like these, they justify violent behavior and create an endless pool of victims.

The line between hoe and "woman" is subjective to whoever wants to justify dehumanization or violence. Anybody can be a hoe. Anybody can be "asking" for it. The woman who has a body count of 9 or the chick with two bodies and unfortunate revenge porn on the timeline. The 9th grader who has a poor reputation because all of the girls in her grade are jealous and mean. This is a particular hardship for black women, who face sexual policing in their music, religion, entertainment, and social environments.

This country has a deeply rooted tradition of classifying black women as jezebels, incapable of being victims. Think about Mrs. Recy Taylor, who was raped by six men in 1944 Alabama. "Nigger ain't $600 enough for raping your wife?" the group's lawyer inquired to her husband Willie while he considered dropping the rape allegation. Most of the men had admitted to raping Recy to the authorities. Before executing the assault at gunpoint, one of the men said: "act just like you do with your husband or I'll cut your damn throat." After the case was dismissed by an all-white jury and a second investigation was launched thanks to efforts from Rosa Parks and others, Recy's name was dragged through the dirt. The local sheriff said she was "nothing but a whore   113 around Abbeville", and claimed that she had been treated for venereal disease before. One of the rapists admitted that they had been out looking for a woman to rape that night. Four of the seven men countered "that she was essentially a prostitute and willing participant" in her attack. The all-white jury for a second time refused to indict.

Many toxic attitudes in the black community are regurgitated leftovers of white supremacy. Too many of our own men can only see us as troublesome, no good, dirty THOTS.... or good, regal, and modest queens. To too many men, there is no gray area, nor any consideration of circumstance or abuse. There are only good women and there are BAD hoes... there are respectable women and there are whores who are ALWAYS asking for it. You'd be a fool to not notice that this idea trickles down to our young girls. The ones called fast. The ones who are told they are asking to be sexually abused because of shapely bodies, thick lips, or age-appropriate interest in the opposite sex. That 50-60 % of black girls who are sexually assaulted by the age of 18. The girls often blamed for their own abuse. These are the girls that nobody cares about exploiting because some men don't treat whores like human beings.

This socialization lies at the intersections of American racism, patriarchy, and classism. This is all alarming and relevant because black females are trapped between being "good women" or whores to so many in our community. Because being a good woman is subjective, the slut-shaming, victim blaming, and misogynistic attitudes we allow to exist unscathed are putting our girls and women at risk. We are projecting an atmosphere of apathy; an atmosphere that permits troubled girls to be snatched up with little alarm. According to an Urban Institute study, sex traffickers operated under the belief that "white women would make them more money but trafficking black women would land them less jail time if caught."

To be clear, all girls of all races are at risk of sex trafficking and it isn't just a black issue. Nor is it alone American issue, as human trafficking is prevalent around the world. But because of the historically rooted tradition of sexually exploiting black women (and ignoring them) in this country, the risk for our girls is intensified. We MUST do what we can to alleviate that risk; beginning with understanding how we contribute to the problem. It isn't enough to be shocked that 64,000 black girls and women are missing right now.

Fast Girls and Good Girls, Hoes and Housewives

In 1967 *The Seventeen Guide to Knowing Yourself* summed up what a fast girl was, with no room for negotiations. She was described as "someone who is using sex to work out problems that have little to do with sex, and her solution only creates deeper problems... It is a fact that most boys lose respect for an 'easy mark' and after a torrid affair are quite likely to decide that the young woman is 'not the kind of girl I want to be the mother of my children'." In just those few sentences, one of the most popular teen magazines at the time captured a national attitude about female promiscuity. It had long been established that promiscuous girls use sex to fill a hole within themselves and will never find love or healthy relationships with men. Fast girls, whether or not they were actually having sex, were not the kind of girls to bring home to mom. They are to be used and tossed to the side like Kleenex. Being a fast girl has historically been a perilous label for women of any color, but as with most things, shit is particularly hard when you're black. Promiscuity and the fast girl label was and has been an entirely different beast for black girls and women because our reputation as insatiable sexpots has preceded us for half a millennia.

I went to a *High School Musical* wannabe institution by the name of Northwest School of the Arts. Highly diverse both racially and economically, it was a 6th-12th-grade school divided into artistic factions, the kind of place where Capezio wearing eighth graders obsessed with Kathryn Graham and Alvin Ailey hung out with Doc Marten-wearing, reefer smoking, paint-speckled 17-year-olds because they were forced to bond in the same torturous elective Drama class. Hardboiled young black men from the hoods of West Charlotte with singing voices of smooth silk brushed shoulders with effeminate white musical theater majors from the luxurious suburbs of South Charlotte. Vegan Sylvia Plath reading emos mingled with the Baby Phat fashionistas saddled with side ponytails and bags of hot Cheetos. Young thespians who had been sent to theater summer camps by their wealthy parents auditioned against ghetto incumbents like me for parts in school productions. The only thing missing from the landscape was athletes, as Northwest had no sports teams of any kind.

It was a sprawling campus with multiple buildings and exits that I eventually found to be excellent in aiding games of hooky. My first day of sixth grade I was astounded to see kids playing musical instruments in the cafeteria and brave souls attempting break dancing 117 routines in the asphalt courtyard. The cafeteria sold iced tea, cheese fries, and Dominos pizza; and if you ask anyone who came out of Charlotte Mecklenburg Schools in the past seven years, those are long forgotten luxuries. Everyone began conversations by asking "What's your major?" Double and triple majors had clout, and were usually excellent drama queens. If you asked anyone what they planned on being when they were older, it often involved being famous. You could take classes on piano, jazz theory, foreign languages, fashion merchandising, and various forms of dance. Every Halloween my dance teacher taught her students the routine to Michael Jackson's *Thriller*.

Because Northwest was dedicated to creativity and individuality, dress codes were non-existent. CMS had extensive rules about how students should dress but none of the administrators at Northwest really gave a fuck. It was a pretty progressive school for a red state like North Carolina. Tall black boys with modern dance honed muscles twisted through the hallways in ripped shirts and tight leggings and nobody gave a second glance. Midriffs were bared, thighs were exposed, and I even witnessed a girl named Ivy stick a safety pin in her lip as an accessory during 2nd-period computer science. The sixth graders were contained to a hallway on the highest floor of the main building when they weren't in the other buildings for their major classes. The hallway was like a runway, with the lockers lined up along the walls and smiling teachers hustling you to class. Between each class period, we had seven minutes to get from place to place, and you better believe every second of those seven minutes were utilized to socialize and be seen. I wince thinking back on the salaciously shitty outfits I wore, clamping down the hallway with ego and pomp. It was a school full of attention lovers (including the visual artists who were usually clad in head-to-toe black and rocking out to System of a Down), and we all did our best to soak it up.

All of the sixth-grade girls knew mostly everyone within their racial groups and major classes, but there was one girl that it seemed everyone knew for sure. The white girls knew her. The black girls knew her. The Spanish girls knew her. Her name was Detria Loudermilk and she was the sixth-grade slut. Detria was pretty, looked foreign (read: mixed), and regularly wore mini skirts with short heels and no tights. I distinctly remember her long brown legs in a short black ruffle skirt, wishing that I could wear an outfit like that and look just as good. The boys loved her. The girls hated her, including me. I was chubby and bespectacled, and Detria represented everything I wanted to be. Soon enough I was whispering about her hoe behavior along with everybody else. I highly doubt Detria did anything us jealous sixth graders claimed she did, but her reputation was sealed for the remainder of the year. Never mind the fact that we all flirted and a lot of us wore skimpy clothes. I remember my outfits. I remember my insecurities. I locked in on a target. I might have considered myself a little quick... but Detria was *fast* (in my head, atleast) She was the bar that I could never topple, thanks to those vicious sixth grade rumors.

I can't speak for everyone, but Detria allowed me to feel good about myself because I wasn't her. She was one of the fast girls my nana and mom had continuously warned me to avoid. "Fastness" was always described as something highly contagious. Associating with her would ruin my own reputation, so I secretly admired 119 her from afar and publicly condemned her like the rest of my friends who'd come to me with the latest gossip. I would never be her. Or so I thought.

I was a seventh grader when I officially became one of the fast girls. It started off innocently enough when I sat on the wrong side of the bus. I had recently moved in with my nana and papa while my mom moved out to Atlanta to prepare a life for me to move to by the end of school year. It was unknown to me at the time, but there was a hierarchy to this new school bus that permeated the daily 40-minute ride across town. On my previous bus, we had seat assignments, and I sat with a 17-year-old girl every day (who eventually began molesting me, but that's a different story). The new bus was completely different. Some of the most popular boys in school rode my bus, and it was much more crowded with high school teenagers than middle school pre-teens. The seats were higher. The bus driver was always cracking jokes with the people who sat in the first few seats, and whatever happened in the back of the bus rarely made it to her consciousness unless it was deathly serious or super funny. When I sat in the middle of the bus towards the back, I had unknowingly chosen the fast girl section. I had been separated into a tainted caste.

A lot happened back there. I learned that I was thick for the first time. I had always considered myself chubby, and the boys in my grade were busy chasing after the lithe dancer girls. A boy whose name I forget told me that I was "thick as fuck". To me, the ugly duckling, it translated to "Wow, you're beautiful." I began looking forward to riding the bus in the afternoon because I was lavished with attention. After being molested in the sixth grade, I felt really guilty about my same-sex feelings. I wasn't even sexually active at that time, and was scared to be called a lesbian. So sitting in the back of the bus became a regular thing. I wanted to prove to myself that I liked boys which wasn't even necessary. I was bursting with hormones and I wanted to interact with boys as much as I could. It never occurred to me until much later that most of the girls sitting toward the back of the bus were of middle school stock. There were three or four high school girls who sat in the middle seats, always looking back at the rest of us with judgmental eyes. By the end of the first month, the sexual politics of the bus were fully understood. The girls in the back were fast.

It all started with what a 17-year-old guy named Todd called *Get in the Game*. When you walked to your seat, the boys would slap your butt and yell "get in the game". They never slapped each other's butts or the good girls in the middle, just the girls in the back. I thought it was funny. I loved the attention, too. I developed a crush on a guy named Chris, who I believe was 15 or 16 His twin sister was one of the girls who sat in the middle seats, never engaging in the debauchery except to add a joke or two. There was always a crazy conversation going on involving jokes or sex, and I remember shrieking with laughter on multiple occasions. I also recall getting roasted for exposing my underarms once in a sleeveless top, where a tiny sliver of black hair had begun growing. "Lexi a hairy bitch!" yelled a popular eighth-grade boy named Nutsack. I was tormented for the rest of the bus ride. I went home and shaved my armpits and vagina immediately The next day at school I winced constantly from razor cuts near my vulva. I could barely take a step that day without hating myself.

It was also on the very back of the bus where I touched my first penis, and it belonged to the 17-year-old Todd, who had begged me to do it after whipping it out and making me look at it. I was trapped in the seat and five minutes away from home. He told me I had "real nice dick sucking lips". I was 12 at the time. When I refused to suck it, he told me I had to touch it or he would tell people I sucked it.

Somewhere in the middle of the year, things got worse when an insane game of *Truth or Dare* landed me into a kiss with Nutsack, who unbeknownst to me had a girlfriend. I went home thinking he liked me. The next morning at school my friend had pulled me to the side and told me all the girls wanted to fight me for sucking Nutsack's dick on the bus. I was incredulous that a simple kiss had, overnight, turned into a blowjob.
It was the 8th-grade girls who allegedly wanted to fight me, as Nutsack's girlfriend turned out to be as popular as he was. I remember walking into the cafeteria to see a sea of eyes staring at me (except for the white kids because they had their own drama going on). Girls who had never noticed me before were now doing so. Boys who had never made eye contact with me were desperately trying to do so. I spotted Nutsack and my heart pulsed with fury. What had he said to people?

As I began to approach him, he stepped backward and put his fingers up in the shape of a cross, repelling me and my evil hoe stench for all to see. It was one of the most embarrassing moments of my life, but the 12-year-old me hoped that he was just joking. After a full two minutes of chasing him around the cafeteria, I realized it wasn't a joke. He was distancing himself from me. I was humiliated, and not quite sure how to snap out of the scene. The mixed crowd of ruthless middle-school-ers and reluctantly interested high-schoolers had tasted blood. From that moment onward, girls distanced themselves from me. I was "that" girl. Rumors flew about who I was stalking, fucking, or trying to fuck... when the truth was that I wasn't fucking anybody except for a girl who lived next door to my nana's house.

The older boys from my bus intensified the rumors. I briefly dated a guy named TJ, who "cheated" on me by the fifth day of our courtship because he was frustrated to find out I actually wasn't having sex. When I got suspended later that school year for fighting and got sent to Derita Alternative School, I returned to Northwest in the fall to rumors that I had dropped out and had a baby. I had very few girlfriends because they didn't want to gain my reputation, and the only people who wanted to talk to me were guys seeking a nut; which of course made girls distance themselves from me even more. After enduring one more year of gossipy torture that my mom eventually heard about through Charlotte's imposing grapevine, I was enrolled at Harding University High School for a fresh start, but to me, the damage seemed to be done. It seemed like everyone else believed I was a vile harlot, so I did too. There was no returning to good girl status. I was a fast girl. I was lost.

The fast girl s always swathed in red flags for others to identify her and label her appropriately. Some of these markers are the results of her own choices- think "grown" hairstyles, "inappropriate for your age" lip and/or nail colors, or "hooker" clothes- but many are out of her control. Boys and men are attracted to her. The girls and women around her notice the boys and men who are attracted to her. She is accused of seducing 123 them or seeking their attention, in the same manner that a black female slave was often accused of seducing or corrupting her sexual abuser. Even if the fast girl is interested in arousing the interest of her male peers- no differently than her nonfast counterparts because that's how hormones work- she is vilified for it and ostracized as a freak. Until recently, the word freak was considered a definite insult. The fast girl commits behaviors in the same fashion as a boy not interested in committing to a relationship, but her assigned gender role as a woman means that she should be aspiring to be in a relationship. If she doesn't want a relationship, she's broken in some way.

If the fast girl has no father figure, she is told by potential and future partners that any romantic torment she endures is because she has daddy issues. Just recently I stumbled upon a twitter user who declared that one should never date a girl with daddy issues, that they're only good for sex because they don't know how to function in real relationships. Fatherless girls are not worthy of love. Wow. What a concept. Perhaps the greatest red flag of a fast girl is her body. Girls with fuller thighs, asses, hips, and lips are often assumed not only to be sexually active but heavily experienced. Even when I was still a virgin who had only experimented with another girl, my body told a different story to the girls and boys around me. To their peers, black girls shaped like black grown women must be getting it in. This is a startling parallel to Europeans who assumed that black women were sexually devious because of their bodacious figures.

A black girl who develops early and attracts the attention of men and boys will find it next to impossible to shake the "fast girl" moniker that later evolves into the "hoe" label. You know the widely accepted version of the hoe because you've seen her in movies and heard about her in songs. She has a lot of guy friends. She sleeps with anyone and everyone. She's probably loud and considered mouthy. She'll sleep with your man. She'll travel a lot. She'll post sexy pictures of herself. She'll cheat on her man. She'll leave her man for cheating, instead of forgiving him. She'll date a man just for money or a free meal. She'll make her own money and only use men for sex. She'll have a lot of kids. She'll have no kids past the expected time to have kids because she doesn't want to settle down. Notice how some of these contradict each other and are not considered irreversible flaws in black men.

At one point the whore talked about in movies and songs was easily defined as a chick who sold pussy. Somewhere along the line it became any black woman who sought too much attention, had too much sex, or embodied any other characteristic that black men didn't like. The mythology of the hoe has grown into something so chameleon-like and multi-faceted that any black girl or woman can be moisturized in its maliciousness. Staying away from the slutty category has historically been important for women of various races in a multitude of cultures, but black girlhood is marred by a special context that makes rejection of hoe-dom crucial. As an adolescent I was always instructed against hanging with fast girls or trying to look fast, despite an innate desire to feel and appear attractive and flirt with my peers. I know I wasn't the only one. Even for the black women who never before heard the term, many have been exposed to the ideology and have spent their lives as if it's a constant audition for marriage.   125

Because finding and keeping a man has proven itself to be an important pillar of black womanhood, many of us heard from early childhood onward on that you can't turn a hoe into a housewife. As rapper Ludacris declared in 1999's *Ho*, "You cant turn a ho into a housewife, hos don't act right, there's hos on a mission and there's hos on a crack pipe."

"Young good looking white women were the most desirable creatures in the world. It was hard not to want to imitate them; it was highly toxic, too; as we would learn," wrote Margot Jefferson in *Negroland*. During the reconstruction period when black women desperately sought a way to curb sexual violence from white and black men alike, respectability politics became a key weapon. Because white women were societal motifs of sexual morality; delicate flowers who were not to be plucked or plundered without express property rights, black women adopted their sexual identity. In doing so, black women rejected the stereotype that they were lascivious and scandalous by embodying the social and sexual traits of the oppressors. This was especially common for the middle and upper-class blacks, whose identities were partly defined by their sense of moral superiority and authority to lower class blacks.

From the desire to gain respectability and protection from sexual assault came the birth of two identities central to black girlhood: the fast girl and the good girl. Presenting a dichotomy of black girlhood and forcing girls to choose between the two is like choosing between a single brown or black colored pencil to color a rainbow: the choices are garbage and the result will be too.

It is no accident or coincidence that the fast girl embodies the traits of the jezebel: seductive, nefarious, selfish, unsuitable for partnership, and most importantly, the inability to be a victim. The fast girl label comes in many flavors; the hoe, the whore, the freak. Because the hoe serves the sexual needs of others, she is disposable. Notice that it is not a common belief that a woman can both love herself AND love to fuck. This tells me that too many of us see sex as something done to women, and not something that women choose to experience for physical pleasure. I don't deny that there are girls and women who seek sexual contact to fill a hole that fatherlessness left them. Instead. I seek to point out that this is not exclusive to female humans.

Many men (with and without mommy issues) sleep around because they crave intimacy. With that being said, the women who sleep around for emotional intimacy aren't always the same women out here chasing orgasms. That shakes some men to their cores. They miss the days when "men were men and women were women." They literally hate the concept of women who have sex without catching feelings and reject it as a possibility. Even though men are authorized to do the EXACT same thing, they call women who have casual sex "hoes" who have no self-respect because it scares them to know that some women are not emotionally minded and easily manipulated.

Being a woman is associated with virtue and motherhood, two things that deserve protection. For whatever reason a girl is a "hoe"- economic coercion, abuse, rumors, the love of fucking- many believe she has forfeited the privilege of being a woman. She does not have self-respect. Because a lot of men claim that hoes don't have self-respect, they think showing respect   127 to hoes is optional. It is disgustingly similar to white supremacists who claim that black people don't respect themselves so they aren't obligated to show any to them. Isn't it a little convenient that the oppressors can opt out of showing you respect because they believe you don't have any for yourself? Who decides what self-respect is, anyway? Isn't it ironic that many black men claim women who have sex with multiple partners have no self-esteem, yet many of those same men validate their own self-esteem and masculinity using the quantity of their sexual conquests? Let's not play coy. If sex wasn't central to black male posturing, a good chunk of rap lyrics wouldn't exist. Lyrics are dotted with similar tales of fucking someones bitch, fucking lots of bitches, being around naked bitches, playing with foreign bitches, and associating with freak hoes. Isn't it hilarious that the same men who rap and idealize these lyrics are often the first to ignore the contributions or achievements of a fast girl or hoe because he believes that she doesn't have respect for herself?

Many Americans have swallowed the public school narrative that a brave woman named Rosa Parks spontaneously refused to give up her seat to a white man on December 1st, 1955 and sparked a boycott that desegregated buses in Alabama. It made for a lovely CBS movie in which Angela Bassett predictably acted her ass off, but it wasn't the truth. The attempt to desegregate Alabama public busses truly began nine months earlier on March 2nd, when sixteen-year-old Claudette Colvin refused to move to the back of a segregated bus. She was arrested, convicted, and fined in a timely fashion. Three more women, Mary Louise Smith, Suzi McDonald, and Aurelia Browder were also arrested and convicted of doing the same thing. These four women later started a suit against the city that ultimately changed the law. If we're being technical, Claudette Colvin began the movement of desegregating Montgomery buses. But when busses were officially desegregated in December 1956, the NAACP asked Rosa Parks, a light-skinned and middle-aged woman to pose for a photograph on a city bus. Claudette, who was one of the four plaintiffs that brought legal action against the city AND the first Montgomery black person to refuse to move from her seat, was left out of the story.

Why? To start, she wasn't the right skin color. In a later interview Claudette noted: "My mother told me to be quiet about what I did. She told me: let Rosa be the one. White people aren't going to bother Rosa- her skin is lighter than yours and they like her." Secondly, many in the movement thought that Claudette was too rowdy, too ghetto, and not relatable enough. "I kept saying, 'He has no civil right... this is my constitutional right... you have no right to do this.' And I just kept blabbing things out, and I never stopped. That was worse than stealing, you know, talking back to a white person," Claudette continued in that same interview. She was actually labeled a troublemaker by those in her community, and eventually had to drop out of school and move to the Bronx. Because of her lack of white and black appeal, she wasn't the NAACP's ideal candidate to lead the boycott movement. There was also another juicy tidbit that kept Colvin from going down in the history books, and likely to be the biggest reason why the black people around her didn't want to rally behind her.

Although Claudette was a member of the NAACP youth organization she was also pregnant with a married man's child. There was also talk that the father of 129 her child was also a white man. There were no attempts to investigate sexual assault or abuse, even though she was 15 and likely to be a victim of a predatory older man or economic coercion. Instead, she has brushed aside because Rosa Parks, an NAACP secretary, was schooled in the art of appearing non-threatening and ultimately respectable.

I'm not saying Rosa Parks' action to refuse to give up her seat was not important, but I am saying that it was a calculated endeavor borne of Claudette's earlier moment. Rosa was already well known and liked in the local black community. With her light skin, community popularity, and lack of sexual skeletons in her closet, Rosa was outfitted as the leader of the boycott movement. Her name is the one spoken when people discuss bus desegregation in Alabama... not Claudette's.

This is despite the fact that a number of historians agree that Montgomery's busses would have been integrated with or without Rosa Parks thanks to the court case that was initiated by Claudette's actions. This harnesses a crucial question: why are the important achievements of females labeled fast girls and hoes discredited or forgotten about? On a personal note, my brief stint as a cam girl was brought to twitters attention after my thread regarding 9/11, black oppression, and white supremacy went viral. I was not ashamed of my past, and made it clear on my twitter page. However I knew it would impact my support and was therefore not surprised when a few men entered my mentions and mockingly asked their followers "is a whore trying to teach people?" It made me wonder how many other women's important work has been devalued due to their lack of status as respectable.

The story of Claudette Colvin illustrates a very important point about the status of fast girls and hoes in the black status quo. Claudette certainly wasn't the first or last black woman to be ejected from the history books for not fitting the respectability mold. Her story is a stark reminder that many people believe hoes are a threat to the black community and our agenda of progression. White judgment is everything. Claudette Colvin was not only the antithesis of a respectable woman to black people, but to white people as well. Black leaders placed Rosa Parks at the head of the movement because she could appeal to the black people concerned with respectability politics and the whites. But the need to appeal to mainstream oppressive ideals for white cool points isn't the only reason why the sexuality of black women has been so regulated. After all, black men enjoy a reputation for being relentlessly sexual that most modern black leaders have not tried to dissolve even after over a century of the black on white rape myth.

On a large scale, black men have not sought to alter their behavior for the sake of not being seen as rapists. Even while family man Martin Luther King Jr. was pushed by the Civil Rights Movement as the antithesis of what America considered to be black sexual deviance, he had several affairs with many women. He was the most famous black man in America and he didn't give a fuck about risking his squeaky clean public image. He was going to get his dick wet, dammit. To ask black men to relinquish their sexual power (so long as its heterosexual) because of how white people see them is rightfully seen as preposterous in our community. We as a majority do not look at the sexually explicit personas of black male celebrities and barrage them with questions about   131 their future children or demand that they be better role models. It is NOT preposterous in our community, however, to ask black women to relinquish their sexual power. This is male privilege, pure and simple. Male privilege allows heterosexual black men to both exercise their sexuality and be productive members of the black community. It makes you wonder how many black women didn't reach their full potential because they weren't the quintessential good girl. How many black girls over the past century were socialized to believe that because they were fast, they could never be meaningfully useful to black progression?

Thanks to patriarchy, heterosexual, cis-gendered black men command the black social scene. Ya'll know I don't deny they are black and therefore oppressed on the basis of race... but they are also men and enjoy the social and economic benefits of being men. Thus, the hoe label is never used as a serious blow to their social or economic reputations. It is one of the few lucky cards that black men have been dealt, in a card game where both white men and women enjoy racial privileges that they do not. This card, enabling their sexual freedom, is one that many black men refuse to ever let black women have... whether they are consciously aware of it or not. Perhaps fellas aren't realizing that they are regurgitating oppressive tactics and ideologies that were used by white men throughout history to subject their black female ancestors to a plethora of horrors. Maybe if more black men knew and understood the history behind the stereotypes they push on black women, they'd be less likely to use them. How is "if a nigger wants respect..." any different from "if a hoe wants respect..."? Many pro-black men acknowledge that white people are uncomfortable relinquishing their privileges, but can't face the same hard truth in their own communities. It has been proven by multiple studies that when men who feel they are losing power, some use violence or the threat of violence to maintain power.

This might explain the hostility men direct towards girls and women who step outside of their gender role from "woman" into "hoe." A 2002 study proved that there was a direct link between the stereotypes of black women and domestic violence. A highly varied sample of black Michigan men was asked a series of questions about their endorsement of the jezebel stereotype and their own histories with domestic violence. 48% of the sample actively endorsed the jezebel stereotype, and men who reported no college education were more likely than men with at least some college education to believe the stereotype. Men who reported no committed relationships that lasted more than three years were more likely to endorse the Jezebel stereotype. Lastly, the justification of domestic violence was strongly tied to those who pushed the jezebel label.

In a nutshell, sexually liberated black women threaten black masculinity. They also threaten the exquisitely sensitive status quo that places hyper-masculine black men at the top of the social rankings on the black totem pole of power. Not every black man gives a fuck about the actions of black women, but those who do make it their mission in life to make women feel lesser than they are. These are men who hate women; also called misogynists. The relationship between the hoe and the misogynist is a precarious one. She both validates his masculinity and jeopardizes it. Black men who measure their masculinity by their sexual conquests have sex with hoes. Black women who have sex with little   133 regard for settling down in a relationship are defying expectations of black femininity defined for them by black patriarchs. They are supposed to want to be mothers, to be wives, to be "good". Think about why whenever a black woman does something considered promiscuous, she is asked what her future children will think.

A good chunk of black women's status in this country was that of forced baby makers, solidifying their primary role of child bearers and stamping out their sexual autonomy. Recall that when a slave woman had a child, it was also a slave. This made her valuable to her masters, as the creators of more labor. Though they didn't always get to raise the child in the same vein of motherhood we have today, at the very least each child was nine months of motherhood that every black female slave experienced. The sex they had was tied to motherhood... whereas black men were just required for the sexual aspect. They didn't carry the child and often never raised the child. Sex was not explicitly tied to fatherhood for them. Because black men had few social, economic, and political validations of their manhood during slavery.... sexual conquests, not fatherhood, became their thing. When black women infringe on one of the few privileges enjoyed by black men in a white mans world, it translates as a loss of power. It is no different than white people who cling to their privileges while denying people of color the same ones. Merge this concept of oppression with white respectability politics and you have generations black of women who have gone to great lengths to never appear promiscuous- because it is their duty to be wives and mothers and not multi-faceted and sexually autonomous beings.

The good girl, constantly aware of the popular and

aforementioned adage "you cant turn a hoe into a housewife", goes hard to never be placed in the fast category. "Fast meant social extermination by degrees because the boys who'd sampled a fast girl would tell another girl they'd taken up with (who was desirable but not fast) that the first girl was a slut." wrote Margot Jefferson in *Negroland*. Most girls want to be the second girl and not the first girl.

Most good black girls are adhering to a religious doctrine, as studies show that black people have a higher rate of religiosity than their peers. The constant battle to be pure (or at least appear to be) can take a toll on a young woman's psyche, self-esteem, and relationships. After all... her reputation hangs on a delicate string that can snap at any time- and rumors, like red wine spilled on a white suede couch, are impossible to scrub away completely. With great care and tremendous luck the good girl tips around the landmines that fast girls can't avoid. Because showing interest in sex is the mark of a fast girl, she represses and feelings or urges until they manifest in guilt or shame. She might feel disgusted with herself after losing her virginity. If she happens to be shapely, she dresses in a way that diverts attention away from her body because developed bodies are a fast girl trait.

Memoirist Anne Moody noted being embarrassed to wear her too tight dresses to school, instead opting to wear jeans as she couldn't afford new clothes. Even those were too tight and made her feel shame. Luckily for her, she said the "faster girls started wearing jeans that were even tighter than mine." Notice how the good girl disassociates from girls who have bad reputations because she doesn't want to become a victim of the 135 popular hoe rhetoric, "birds of a feather flock together." Anne continued to state that "All the girls...were split into two groups, the fast and the quiet."

Girls were and still are forced to choose between two types of girlhood with detrimental results. When the good girl has a sex question, she's less likely to ask an authoritative source because she doesn't want to be seen as fast. This could include crucial questions that are less about sex and more about how her own body works. In states where schools give abstinence-only education, the chances of a good girl getting STDs and becoming pregnant when she eventually has sex are even higher. As of 2014, black teens aged 15-19 are 12.7% more likely than white teens to have gonorrhea. Black women are 5.7% times more likely to have chlamydia. Black women are infected with HIV at a higher rate than any other group.

Because they're too embarrassed or prideful to seek out valid information, they are more likely to be blighted in their sexual experiences. When you pair this with the systematic disadvantages that many black girls face- limited health care access, limited school funding for health programs, and limited access to cheap birth control- it is easy to see why the fast girl rhetoric is so much more damaging for black girls. The less sexual education they have, when compounded with common attitudes about sex in the black communities, trap them in a cycle filled with racial disadvantages. When these women fall victim to preventable STD's and pregnancies, they miss more socio-economic opportunities and then become the mothers of the next generation of children trapped in the same cycle.

Another horrifying component of the good girl/fast girl dichotomy is the belief that fast girls are asking for sexual abuse. A 2007 study showed that black women are less likely to disclose their sexual assaults and less likely to receive support when they did disclose. A quick scroll on Twitter will confirm that many black men and women alike don't show the most support for victims of sexual assault. Common rebuttals for victims include analysis of their sexual pasts or reputations. Were you asking for it or nah? Perhaps the most dangerous and depressing aspect of the plight of the good girl is her likeliness to blame herself if she's ever sexually assaulted... particularly if she is growing up in poverty or receives a minimal education. Because the good girl does not actively seek out information on sexual health or education, she is more likely to believe sexual assault myths than more educated women. Multiple studies show that less educated black women are more likely to blame themselves for sexual assault instead of their attacker.

But good black girls aren't the only ones at higher risk of being sexually assaulted. Remember who fast girls evolve into. Hoes. Nasty women who one can do anything to with little fear of repercussion. This is the part where some of the guys reading this passage will stop to tweet me that they don't believe in calling women hoes, or that they treat all women with respect. That's excellent. But I'm not talking about you. There are many black men out there who do believe that women categorized as hoes are less than human. In addition to being at the receiving end of "hoe treatment" by men who would cry if their mothers were treated in the same manner, I've seen the tweets, blog posts, song lyrics, and news headlines for myself... as have other women.   137

Even some black scholars show disgust at black women who display sexual agency because they claim that doing so feeds the stereotype of black female hypersexuality. When you dismiss the very important conversation that needs to be had about how sexually liberated women of color are perceived and treated in our community, you are helping uphold a system of abuse and pain that has accompanied our women since the establishment of American slavery.

Often women who fulfill the "hoe" role haven't necessarily chosen this label as much as they have been boxed into it since childhood era forces beyond their control. As a child, she was likely labeled fast. Whether she developed early, didn't have a father figure, or attracted the attention of male peers, she had no choice in these matters- though they still became signals of her promiscuity to others. Any normal thoughts she had about sexuality were distorted as devious. Any sexual assaults she experienced from older men or peers was blamed on her low self-esteem (and therefore her fault). Any normal sexual experiments she performed were purported as obvious signs of her moral deficiency.

Anne Moody summed up the common attitude of the 1940s: "The young white housewife didn't dare leave [a negro girl] alone in the house with her loyal and obedient husband. She was afraid that the Negro girl would seduce him, never the contrary." The large-scale sexual assault of black women was justified by their European bestowed reputation of insatiable lust; only enriched by the woes of slavery. So today, there are black people who believe that when a black woman is overtly sexual she is proving the jezebel stereotype to be true. Continued Margo Jefferson, "Premature sexual activity and pregnancy out of wedlock? She was just another statistic to be held against the race." Today, these attitudes have not gone away. It's why you see memes that say "There are too many Nicki Minajs and not enough Michelle Obamas!" There are plenty of people in our community who believe that a black sexually liberated woman is nefarious (to be hated), insatiable (to be taken advantage of), and less than human (to be treated however).

That's fucking ridiculous. Black women are humans with sexual needs and desires just like black men, white men, and everyone else (save for the asexuals). By denying black women sexual agency on the belief that their sexual liberation gives white people a valid reason to keep stereotyping our community, you are doing two things. Primarily you are seeking the approval of white people, reeking of the respectability politics that have held us all back for centuries. Secondly, you are not only refusing that black women are equally capable of sexual autonomy and self-love but refusing the notion that black women can be both sexual AND productive members of the black community. You are forcing them to choose one. You are saying that there are only fast girls and good girls.

When my fate as the fast girl was sealed in middle school, I became lost in the notion that I would never be more than someone's whore. It took me three years to wiggle my way out of the hole I believed I was supposed to be in. Because I was not good I was bad by default. My thoughts and actions no longer catered to my own beliefs, but to the image people had boxed me into.

When you call a black woman a whore for seeking

sexual pleasure or even just human interaction via thirst trap, you are tucking us all back into the category of jezebel... a category born of racial oppression and sexual abuse. It's sad that I have to even say this but think of your girlfriend, your sisters, your aunts, your cousins, or your mom. Because a hoe can be a woman who participates in gangbangs, goes bra-less, dates more than one man at a time, or who has slept with a guy since breaking up with her long-term boyfriend (to his chagrin and jealousy), any woman is at risk. Your girlfriend, your sisters, your aunts, your cousins, or your mom. When you regularly assign women to a category where the members are widely seen as unworthy of respect and insatiable in their lusts, they are left vulnerable to sexual assault and violence by those who think hoes are for the taking. Your girlfriend, your sisters, your aunts, your cousins, or your mom. This is horrifically congruent to the white slave master's justification of sexually attacking slave women because they wanted to. You are mirroring the oppressor by placing a woman's value in her pussy and telling her that she is worthless if she uses it in a way that you don't approve. You are trash.

Hotep Sex

If anyone can guarantee my fickle body complete and earth-shattering orgasms it is this man. The types of orgasms that leave my cheeks glazed in tears and my body shaking like ass at Magic City. It didn't start out that way, though. Our first encounter was in high school, his dick in my mouth in a broom closet. We had sex on another day when we had access to a condom, and it was lackluster. He graduated that year and I started my junior year at Garinger. We stayed in touch, always meeting up for a session or two when he came home from school. There was always limited talking, and I did know he wanted to be a dentist. But our "friends with benefits" relationship was mainly benefits. We certainly didn't hang out after sex, or cuddle. That's the way I

141

liked it.

I went off to college and we stopped fucking during my junior year, as I rarely came home and I began a monogamous relationship. I didn't really miss it, as college had matured my sexual tastes. Fast forward to spring of this year. I was in Charlotte and single, horny, and stressed. I slid into his direct messages almost as fast as he slid into my crevices. He had grown up and so had his skills. With a few directions, he was soon playing my body like it was a guitar and he was Jimi Hendrix. His powerful sex would render me exhausted, and I began lounging around after our trysts instead of leaving or politely kicking him out of my home. Suddenly I didn't mind cuddling with him after sex. I enjoyed rehashing what went down and didn't hurry through an excuse to kick him out. It wasn't long before I got comfortable. But I soon regretted our post-sex cuddling and conversations.

It all began during a conversation on racism when I mentioned the importance of African history.

"Yeah. They don't want us to know Egypt was the start of civilization." he declared, nuzzling his face into my flesh.
I froze.
Could it be? Did he just-
"After all, white people are scared because they know melanin is magic."
Oh shit. He's a-
"White people are fucking mutants. Demons. We are the supreme beings of earth."
Hotep.

And like a twisted avalanche that could not be stopped,

he piled onto me one pussy parching idea after another.
I only interjected with delicately skeptical questions,
desperate to find out that he was joking. Each question
just led to a different jaw-dropping statement.

"I ain't homophobic, we just gotta put black rights before
all that gay shit'
"They pushing that gay shit on kids."
"Aw Lex you on that feminist wave? Feminists are just trying to take all the power from men, it ain't about equality."
"I mean, I'm not exactly Christian but we are God's chosen
people."
"Farrakhan would have been a good leader if he wasn't on
that Muslim shit
"Man PLEASE tell me you've seen Hidden Colors!"

Mostly everything he said are things often flung in my
mentions by disciples and admirers of the Taric Nasheed and Umar Johnson set. The polite thing to call them
would be black nationalists. I call them hoteps. Black
men (and also black women) who tell me I'm a queen
when I discuss racism but call me a negro bed wench or
traitor for critiquing misogyny in the black community.
They mirror their oppressors when expressing that they
want women to be under men, and when they alter
history to present a narrative that black people are the
superior race. More often than not they have misinformed, hyperbolic, or deliberately wrong ideas about
African history and racism in the United States. Some
hoteps believe ancient Africa to be a monolithic entity,
that Margaret Sanger started Planned Parenthood with
the intention of genociding the black race through abortion, that black women were brainwashed into feminism
by white women, and even that the first president of 143

our country was a black man.

Hoteps and their treatment of black women (or beliefs about how they should function within the black progression movement) is stunningly similar to that of black male leaders during the 1960s and 70s. What goes unmentioned by even the most well-intentioned black people when discussing the Black Panthers was the misogyny within the party and at the hands of its leaders. Eldridge Cleaver, Minister of Information, was a rare find in any time period by any race: he was an admitted rapist. "Rape was an insurrectionary act. It delighted me that I was defying and trampling upon the white man's law, upon his system of values, and that I was defiling his women—and this point, I believe, was the most satisfying to me because I was very resentful over the historical fact of how the white man has used the black woman. I felt I was getting revenge," Cleaver wrote in his autobiography, *Soul on Ice*. Before raping white women, he got his practice by raping black women. Huey Newton authorized the vicious beating of Regina Davis, a Panther Liberation School administrator who had chastised a male subordinate.

"A woman in the Black Power movement was considered, at best, irrelevant. A woman asserting herself was a pariah. If a black woman assumed a role of leadership, she was said to be eroding black manhood, to be hindering the progress of the black race. She was an enemy of the black people.... I knew I had to muster something mighty to manage the Black Panther Party," wrote former Black Panther member and chairperson Elaine Brown in her memoir, *A Taste of Power*. Black Panther women were instructed to "shoot as well as cook," meaning they were expected to be revolutionary and still fulfill traditional gender roles. This attitude initially led to a gender hierarchy in several branches of the party. When Elaine Brown was chairperson of the party after 1974 and ⅔ of the party was made up of women, men who had not been jailed, exiled, or killed often remained in the ranks with resentment.

There are numerous testimonials that assert that there was physical, verbal, and sexual abuse of female panthers at the hands of male members. But it went unaddressed on a wide scale. Elaine Brown explained that like most of her female peers she was turned off by white feminism that centered gender concerns over race and capitalism. She felt compelled to place gender on the back burner and chose to ignore most acts of abuse towards her fellow female Panthers. That was until Regina Davis was beaten up on Huey's orders. Elaine confronted Newton, who had been lodging complaints from male members who felt emasculated while he was in exile, and he ultimately sided with them. Elaine left the Panthers rather than confront the misogyny within.

Quite often hoteps are willing to excuse or ignore the subjugation of Black women with a series of excuses or redundant questions. The three most popular are:

1.   Are you black or a woman first?
2.   Why are you trying to divide us?
3.   Black women cannot be the leaders of this movement because America is a patriarchal society.

The last one is particularly hurtful because it is a direct indication that the person saying it is not interested in equality between the sexes. Instead of us equally fighting for black progression, hoteps insist on a gender hierarchy. In a twisted way, they paint an ideal where black women are somehow hurt less by the battle for progression and power, and also attain less of both. With men in charge of the movement, women's issues fall between the cracks.

There are hoteps who openly claim to have aligned ideals with alt-right white nationalists, who are particularly fond of "good family values" in addition to racism. At the core of their relationship is extreme masculinity and hatred of what they see as genocide against their respective races by way of women's liberation and LGBT rights. Modern white American racists, like every other group of white racists to exist before them here and in Europe, are terrified of becoming the minority. In 1980, white people were 80% of the population. Today, they are 63%. By 2053, they will be a minority. After initially being cool with eugenics and widespread sterilization (including white people who were deemed mentally, physically or morally unfit), the prevalence of black liberation and latino immigration during the 1960s and 70s put the fear of God into whites concerned about the state of the status quo. The word "diversity" to the average white man means black dick in white women. Going hand in hand with the widespread fear of miscegenation was the increase of immigration. Next, the women's liberation movement meant more white women could have fewer children or skip motherhood altogether. As such, white babies are a hot commodity in the minds of white supremacists who disguise themselves as pro-life conservatives.

In these circles, women are expected to do both their gender and race's duties by having lots of babies just in case there is ever.... you know, a race war. A 2016 study of Donald Trump's twitter feed during the primaries showed that 62% of the people he retweeted were ardent supporters of white genocide conspiracy theories. These white genocide conspiracists ultimately desire to keep their women barefoot and pregnant. They want them to fulfill traditional gender roles as women who rely on men to regulate their choices and behavior. They push motherhood as the ultimate sacrifice for the white race, and this is where many hoteps meet white racists on the same level when they try to regulate the reproductive rights and sexual choices of black women under the guise of racial advancement or empowerment.

I'm sorry, but there is nothing empowering about some of my counterparts telling me that my biggest contribution to the movement is my ability to have children. I am not impressed by the shackles of childbirth that my ancestors wore, when having as many babies as possible meant more valuable fieldhands. Nor is it empowering that I am encouraged to stand behind men while they fight instead of standing beside them. I've been told to "let men speak" and to "put your race before your gender". I've been told that my sexual liberation is destroying the black family. I've been told that my criticism of toxic masculinity impairs the black man's ability to grapple racism. I have been told that my sexuality is apart of an agerda in existence to soften, and eventually eradicate, the black man.

On and on the list goes of things I have been told to temper so that the community stands united against racism under the helm of strong black men who will allegedly have everyone's best interests at heart. Strong black men who despite rejecting and/or subjecting black women, gays, transpeople, and other mar-   147 ginalized black groups on their journey to full social, economic, and political power to whites) will allegedly let their power trickle on down to the rest of us. "When racism is conquered, then we can deal with sexism and homophobia," some hoteps claim. "We just have to replace the white man." Chew on that for a moment. Many of them just want to replace the white man- not topple the sexist culture that gives the white man half of his privileges.

As my fuck buddy lay across my breast, my desire to educate him overpowered my urge to slap the stupid out of him. So I began employing the same strategy I've become known for on Twitter. I gave him an entire lecture. His pitiful line of cross-examination to my lecture was crushed with facts and frustrated smacks to my own thigh. When I was done, he looked invigorated, as if he was rethinking everything. He also looked embarrassed, as I had asked him to tell me how many other countries are in Africa aside from Egypt (he hadn't been able to answer). It was in that moment that I realized two things: one, there is probably a business to be had in nude academic lectures. Two, I really cared about whether he had internalized what I said. Particularly the parts about sexism being akin to racism, Africa is a complex and vast region with clashing cultures long before Europeans arrived, and that nobody knows when the fuck Dr. Umar Johnson's school (which he collected hella money for) is being built. I was optimistic and tingly. I only felt that way three times before, each when I was speaking with groups of North Carolina teens about racism and classism.

I shouldn't have placed my hopes so high, however. The next time we fucked the sex was just as good as always.

As I laid in my usual post orgasm trance, he sat up and turned the tv channel. I was glad. The last thing I wanted was to talk. In fact, I was ready to go again. But he had other plans. He cuddled into me "We have a special relationship," he said. I almost dry heaved. This was new territory. "We fuck." I corrected him. "Yeah I know, but we been at it since high school." he retorted. Instead of speaking I recalled a once benign and suddenly terrifying memory from just a few months ago:

> The room is dark except for the light from a TV playing A Pup Named Scooby Doo. The couple is in missionary, but one of the woman's legs is pushed back so that her ankle rests near her ear. He has a hand wrapped around her throat. The only sounds are the woman's moans and sheathed dick sliding into a slowly erupting pussy. "I love this dick." the woman calls out. She cums. "I love this pussy!" the man says. He slams into her twice more. "I love you!" he calls out.

I snapped back into the present with a frightening speed, gaining comprehension of the monologue he was now making. "You're not like these other females! You're actually smart! You not tryna be on that easy money wave either!" Before I could interject, he launched into a speech on how girls from our high school were stripping. He wrapped up his thesis on how strippers were ruining the black community by calling me wifey material. I stared at him, disgust dripping from my face. Was he trying to woo me? I politely reminded him that we once had a threesome (the less evolved call it a train) during my senior year of high school, just to rattle him. "That's different than being out here naked for everybody to see," he countered. So I explained to him the rela- 149 tionship between sex work and capitalism, before telling him that I was a cam girl in college so that I could save money for post-grad and begin writing my first book. I got a sick pleasure watching him grapple with this reality in his head. He said nothing as I grabbed a condom and began massaging his dick, ready for more. When we finished, I got dressed. As I did, I told him to research wealth disparity, to go to my website, and to ask me if he needed any reading recommendations. Again I felt hopeful that whatever brainwashing he had undergone would begin to reverse.

The first time hoteps flooded my mentions, I engaged their questions. By the 9th or 10th flooding, I realized that it was some of the same profiles asking questions I had already answered. Even after I made detailed threads and videos. It seemed like they were deliberately missing the point. So I reluctantly began blocking them instead of trying to educate.

I seriously hoped that my hotep lover was trying to learn.

The next and last time we fucked, I couldn't help but hope that he wouldn't say anything else misogynist or homophobic. In fact, I hoped he wouldn't say anything at all. On Twitter, I block people for saying the vile things that he did. I was angry at myself for allowing our beautiful and mostly physical relationship to erode into a verbal one with opposing views. The sex was not THAT good to where I'd ignore that he believed there is a conspiracy to turn black men gay. Or that he believed black women should behave a certain way for basic respect. Or that he believed white people are our inferiors (a direct regurgitation of how white racists see us). Or that he thought black men, no matter the crime, should never go to prison.

But here I was, back for more of that good ass sex. He was reliable, STD free, and discreet. I had groomed him and his dick to fit my body like a glove. So good was my hotep lover at intensifying my orgasms that he once told me that each time he fucked me he felt like he was reaching a new level in a video game. I didn't want to date him, I just wanted to continue having mindblowing sex with him. Plus, it wasn't like he beat me, put me in danger, or mistreated me. This is what I told myself on the drive over to his house. How badly I wanted the sweet release of non-vibrator induced orgasm.

Moments after he came, I sat up and reached for my phone and shorts. I was determined to avoid conversation, like it was the old days. But it's almost as if he was ready to rumble. Again he pressed me about black feminists and the gay agenda, before reiterating a previous claim that white people were mutants. When I angrily explained to him that he sounded like white people who thought they were superior to blacks, he didn't like that. His next question hit me like a bag of bricks. "You're not all black are you?"

I reeled. It is my guess that my intellect had brought him to that point, where all he had left was to question the authenticity of my blackness. I had patiently answered his questions about toxic patriarchy, misogynoir, and the fundamentals of world history. I offered sources. I carefully challenged each of his misogynistic, homophobic, or supremacist views with easily verifiable facts. I had virtually shat on everything he believed, foolishly thinking that we were both mutual critical thinkers   151 who desired to know all the facts, not just the ones we liked. It dawned on me then that there was no changing his mind or educating him.

Why?

His mind was was not open and he did not want to be educated. He wanted to not only be right but to justify the marginalization (or complete erasure) of black queers and women. He wanted to gain the benefits of white supremacy while being black. His beliefs- that black people are superior to whites and women should be subservient to men- are based in his reality as a black man. Like we all do to some degree, he easily perceives injustices against himself but can't place his feet in another's shoes. And that's my problem with hoteps. All too often they forgo empathy and reality for their [admirable] desire of progression of the black race, because said desire comes with the condition that patriarchy remains intact. Too often they mirror the oppressors in their direct dismissal of facts, their double standards for male behavior, and in their contempt for black women who do not fit their respectability politics.

Every time a hotep finds himself in my twitter mentions, I decide whether or not to block them. I ask myself whether or not they're saying homophobic or misogynistic things to tick me off or if they truly believe all black people's problems will be solved by mimicking the oppressor. After all, I myself said a lot of problematic shit back in the day before people took the time to correct and teach me. So I try not to block them. Every now and then, if I'm bored, I'll indulge their questions or reiterate a point I've made before, just in case they never saw it. There have been times that I get people to concede in my mentions, where they then realize they have more in common with the oppressors than they'd like to admit. Those are the times when the petulant questions and deliberate ignoring of posted links is worth it. But more often than not, engaging with hoteps rewards me with nothing but disappointment. There is no getting them to see that claiming black people are superior to white people is disgustingly congruent to white supremacist rhetoric. There is no enlightening them on the parallels between racism and sexism because they either don't give a damn or have convinced themselves that there aren't any. Like my former lover, their minds are already made up.

Are You TOO Pro-Black?

If you stumble down a certain rabbit hole on twitter, you will encounter a menagerie of declarations that make black people sound divine and perfect. Black women who eat the right diets don't get periods. Homosexuality didn't exist in Africa before Europeans. All African people were kings and queens. Black people, because of our melanin, can cure AIDS with vegan diets. The list of shocking claims goes on and on, hawked by pro-black people who have convinced themselves that black folks are more than human. Tightening their leash of respectability politics around black people who dare to exist outside of Tariq Nasheed and Umar Johnson pedaled mandates of acceptable black behavior, I'm left with the epiphany that some of you motherfuckers are *too* pro-black.

While racists reduce black people to less than human, the too pro-black person has elevated our status to more than human. At the core of their deluded and distracting convictions is the blame of white people for every single problem in the black community. True pro-black people are not interested in excuses or "looking bad" in front of white people. But the *too* pro-black? "They want you to be this divisive, queen," exclaim multiple tweeters in my mentions when I trot out domestic violence and sexual abuse stats in our community. Other men say, "White folks probably getting a laugh out of you attacking us like this." You know all the predictable soundbites. "The black family is being ruined by effeminate men and thots," they tweet, but rarely mention things like the high prevalence of domestic homicide among black women. With these statements in tow, they readily ignore domestic violence, sexual assault, and homophobia among our own people, often only finding the time to comment on police brutality, black women seduced by white feminists, and the gay agenda.

The *too* pro-black person focuses their assault on white people in a way that denies accountability for predators and ner-do-wells in our community. The danger in blaming white people for everything without examining our own behaviors means the same bullshit keeps happening. Accountability is key to progression, especially when it comes to domestic and sexual violence in our community. True pro-black people know that you can both advocate against police brutality and justice system corruption AND come to the objective conclusion that Bill Cosby is a serial rapist. Or that OJ Simpson murdered 155 two people. Or that Chris Brown is physically and emotionally abusive. Or that R Kelly, an adult, had sex with and peed on teenage girls. Or shit, even that Michael Vick participated in some pretty atrocious animal cruelty. This is where someone pauses to ask why I haven't listed any black celebrity women and accuses me of trying to humiliate black men in front of white people. The things is, if there were black female celebs getting away with domestic and sexual violence, I'd mention them. But they aren't. Also, mentioning violence of women when I'm discussing the systematic violence of men is a deflection method employed by white people when rejecting the horrors of slavery or racism. You know, like when you're talking about black lives matter and Hannah or Brad chimes in "But ALL lives matter."

The *too* pro-black is entangled in cognitive dissonance. They mistrust science and statistics that poke holes in declarations of black superiority (or rejections of toxic masculinity). Have you ever met a man who said black men were genetically unable to rape because of their superiority to innate white deviance? I have. Even when Bill Cosby admitted on record to giving potent drugs to women for the purpose of having non-consensual sex with them, *too* pro-blacks continued to say he was being framed. Extremes suck. Extremes disregard circumstances and reality. Racists are incapable of seeing black people as humans or victims. *Too* pro-blacks are incapable of seeing black people as capable of the same atrocities as their oppressors, or as anything but victims who can't be held accountable. Both groups are on the same team, holding black people back from true progression.

Bill Cosby, R. Kelly, and Ruining the Black Man's Legacy

I can recall multiple conversations I had with black men about the Bill Cosby scandal when it was unfolding on the national stage. Some expressed shock. Others recalled a few lines from a stand-up routine, admitting they believed him to be guilty. Most steadfastly denied that he had ever raped anyone. "They just tryna ruin another black man's legacy," they'd declare. Others pitched conspiracy theories about the scandal being revenge for Cosby attempting to buy NBC. But one particular group stood out later when Cosby's mistrial occured in June. There were men, like an acquaintance of mine, who believed Cosby was guilty but celebrated his escape from justice as payback for all the fake rape accusations that occurred against black men throughout history. A couple months later during the Harvey Weinstein revelations, I watched black men on Twitter wonder why many black women did not passionately rebuke Weinstein the way they did Cosby.

Anita Hill was thirty-one years old when she accused Supreme Court Justice nominee Clarence Thomas of sexual harassment in 1991. They were both black. She was single. He was forty-three and married. She was born a poor child of 13 in Oklahoma but clawed her way up to Yale Law where she earned a Juris doctor degree and began her law career in 1980. He started out a poor child of three in Georgia but moved in with wealthy grandparents at the age of 7. He went to an all-white high school and was often the token black, even later in seminary school. Thomas was a controversial selection by George Bush Sr. when Thurgood Marshall retired. Bush was concerned with maintaining the racial quota of one black judge, but he also wanted someone conservative. Clarence had the total Uncle Tom vibes going for him, as his libertarian leanings placed the blame of black suffering on black people's unwillingness to work hard. "I don't believe in quotas. America was founded on a philosophy of individual rights, not group rights," he once said. The Senate judiciary committee split its vote.

Shortly after, Anita Hill revealed that the Supreme Court nominee had committed "behavior that is unbefitting an individual who will be a member of the court." She had followed Clarence from a previous office, claiming to have endured the harassment because she wanted to keep her job. In a world where 98% of the Senate was male, this is understandable. Ultimately Anita was not believed by the Senate and Clarence Thomas went on to be named Supreme Court Justice. I don't want to focus on the he say/she say aspect of the scandal, but I briefly want to scrutinize how Anita Hill was lampooned as not only crazy but as a vindictive and bitter black woman who wanted to see her own fail. As Patricia Hill Collins asked in her book *Black Sexual Politics*, "Why did so many African Americans join the 'fourteen white men dressed in dark gray suits' and reject Hill's allegations of sexual harrasment?" Clarence called Anita's allegations a lynch hunt, which crafted a narrative that invoked the historical image of the black man falsely accused of rape. This was a big no-no in a time purported to be post-racial. Not believing Clarence Thomas meant that you were being racist.

The main fearful claim of southern racists in the post-Civil War era was a regurgitation of old thoughts: that black men were inherently attracted to white women... but with a new twist. Because black men were now free from white control, they would terrorize the south in an effort to taint the white race. White America's disgusting habit of falsely accusing black men of rape has created a quagmire only thickered by the fact that actual white predators often go unpunished. "White men get away with that shit all the time," said my former hotep lover whose sentiments were echoed by countless people on my twitter and facebook timelines. Regardless of what white men do, where is the accountability for black male predators? When I ask this, I'm often met with accusations of hating the black man and seeking his eradication.

But that's the furthest thing from the truth. Is it really so hard to grasp that my love for black men means   159 that they have the ability to hurt my feelings in ways white men never could? The white man is not my counterpart. I do not love white men, expect to marry one, or raise one. I don't want the best for them or care about them evolving into the best versions of themselves. With that being said, a white predator is gross but a black predator hurts my feelings. Am I truly the enemy because I believe the misogyny and rape culture of white men shouldn't be the standard for which black men gauge their behavior?

Robert Kelly was twenty-four years old when he met a 12-year-old aspiring singer named Aaliyah Haughton. At the time he was sleeping with 15-year-old Tiffany Hawkins. Three years later, he married Aaliyah after a frantic phone call from her about a possible pregnancy. Even though it was annulled approximately six months later, the news wasn't shocking to those who knew of Kelly's exploits around Chicago. He apparently had a thing for meeting teens, and the years that followed would prove no different. There was the 17-year-old he impregnated and gifted with an abortion. There were the pictures cops found in 2002 of Kelly having sex with what appeared to be underage girls. Unfortunately, they were obtained during an illegal search and weren't allowed to be leveled in any charges against the *Age Aint Nothing But a Number* singer.

Then, of course, there was the infamous tape of a urinating Robert and his alleged 14-year-old goddaughter. The man in the tape was identified as Kelly, but as the alleged victim refused to testify or confirm her identity (despite several family members and friends who did), he was allowed to walk. Robert's own brother believed he was guilty. In the recent months, Kelly has been accused of operating a sex cult with vulnerable and sometimes underage girls. Despite all of this, there are plenty of people in our community who believe rejecting R. Kelly (or even just critiquing his behavior) is a war cry against the black man.

In the past, white men were the primary rapists and assaulters of black women. Today, black women are more likely to be raped or assaulted by black men, due to proximity. Our female ancestors could not report white men to the authorities because they legally could not do so or because they would face a backlash. When they faced abuse at the hands of black men, they also often suffered in silence.

Today it's a similar tale. We often don't publicly accuse rapists or abusers because we don't want our men thrown in jail. "You don't want to see another black man in jail, do you?" are oft-repeated words. As strong black women, we are supposed to be down for our men in the face of the racist justice system. We are supposed to protect them. But who is protecting black women from domestic violence or sexual assault at the hands of black men- or even attempting to talk about it? Even when given the chance to do so during pop culture abuse scandals, the bulk of our community does the "keep it in the family" approach- where we disapprove quietly but publicly protect black celebs from any criticism that seems to support the stereotype of the black rapist or brute.

Part of what makes celebs and rich black people so central to our culture is that they are symbolic of triumphing against racism. Most white Americans do not look at white celebrities and see their achievements as racially significant. They do not automatically feel the need 161 to jump to the aid of a white celebrity, or feel compelled to protect their honor as good, successful white legends just being brought down by "the man". But black people? Our celebs are sacred because their journeys to fame and success are often paved with discrimination and malice. In many of our minds, we are thinking white America didn't want them to win but they did anyway. And on a simpler level, some of us place entertainment before human decency. So we coddle them and ignore their worst behavior. I mean, am I right? Who gives a fuck if a grown man preyed on teens and peed in a girls mouth? *Ignition Remix* is a bop!

The thing is, if rich white Ben at Hedgefund Inc openly did all the things that R. Kelly has done to black girls, would our community give him endless excuses or benefits of the doubt? The answer is hell no. We would rightfully malign him as a predator and root for his inevitable foul treatment in prison. We would call him out for treating black women as sexual property in the same way as white slave masters.

But R. Kelly is a black man, not a white guy. Take everything you know about how rich people in America are afforded extra benefit of the doubt. Sprinkle in the power of patriarchy. Now think racially. Because we value black legends in the face of adversity (and live vicariously through their success), we brush off even the foulest of their behavior and vow to forgive. We offer excuses. Take the ever-evolving list of black athletes and celebs who physically abused their lovers. When we let it go unpunished among celebrities, we promote an air of permissiveness among us regular folks too. This all rests on our generational traumas of seeing black men dragged off to jail or murdered for criminal charges. During my senior year of college, I remember a friend of a friend refusing to call the police on the father of her child after he gave her a black eye and held a knife to her throat. "I can't send another black man to jail," she hiccupped through tears, simultaneously fearing for and fearing the man who beat her until she was bloody.

The Black Church [The Good, The Bad, & The Ugly]

Disclaimer #1- "Black Churches" is an umbrella term. It is not meant to be monolithic. The thousands of black churches that have and continue to exist on American soil were carved by regional differences. At no point in the following paragraphs do I mean to imply that every black church is the same. Instead, I want to talk about the many similar aspects of black church culture that have impacted our collective experiences.

Disclaimer #2- White churches are not immune from the bad and the ugly mentioned in these paragraphs, but as a black woman my concern lies with black church culture and its effects on my people.

I was 12 or 13 years old when I began hating going to church. Before puberty, I was a good Christian girl who liked going to Sunday school and adored her 400-page tome of children's bible stories.   said my prayers nightly and I honestly believed that God would make me choke on my food if I didn't say grace. When my attraction to girls became radically clear around the age of 9, I prayed to God to take my affliction away. Not wanting to be doomed to the fiery pits of hell, I revved up my dedication to him. A few friends and associates from sixth grade remember my desire to be a preacher, and my annoying habit of pointing out sin or reciting biblical verses.

On the outside, I was a passionate Jesus freak. On the inside, I was bursting with questions. Questions with answers that the church couldn't provide. Soon after, my Southern Baptist church became a sweatbox of guilt and confusion. These two things eventually gave way to skepticism Everything changed. I despised waking up early on Sundays, abhorred sitting still and listening to sermon for two hours (more if the preacher was feeling frisky), and I absolutely loathed lingering in the church parking lot after service. I'd encounter snooty gossip, noxious cigarette smoke, and sneaky side-eyes between cliques of women doling out Fashion Fair coated smiles. I often wiggled out of too tight hugs from the deacon, who always supplied pocket candy to all the little girls, his friendly forehead kisses just a little too wet and a little too frequent.

My mom didn't go to church regularly, but once or twice a month she'd corner me on a Saturday night with those devastating words. "We going to church tomorrow." Eventually, I was too old to be dragged to church, eyes rolling and chest heaving with boredom. I made sure to work eight-hour shifts on Sunday when I began working at a grocery store at 15, and that was that. I haven't been back to church since. At no point in the past eight years have I desired to enter one, either. When I'm feeling lonely, sad, or broke, the thought of church does not cross my mind. In the black community, I am a minority.

According to the Pew Research Center, 78% of black Americans belong to a Protestant church. 59% belong to historically black churches, like the African Methodist Episcopal Church and the National Baptist Convention. These entities have survived years of racial warfare, serving as battlegrounds and healing wards for our people when no other places would. The First African Baptist Church is believed to be the oldest black place of worship in America, getting its start in Savannah, Georgia in 1777. A smattering of other black churches existed later throughout the lower states, terrifying white southerners with every meeting held within their walls. This fear was rooted in the threat of insurrection from blacks, and it drove many southerners to control what access slaves had to safe black spaces. So many slaves were forced to go to white churches with their masters and made to stand in the back, absorbing lessons about being obedient and good. Others were visited by designated black preachers who delivered special sermons that emphasized rewards for pain in the after-life. In the north, segregated white churches created the need for black ones.

In 1808, black Americans and Ethiopian merchants established the Abyssinian Baptist Church in New York after being discriminated against in a white church. In the post-antebellum, numerous black congregations broke off from integrated churches to do their own thing. Black churches granted agency and freedom, at least within their hallowed halls. Black Americans could now worship where they saw fit- and black churches became more popping than ever. Black people no longer had to sit in the back, or in the rafters. In the south, they were no longer forced to listen to messages about accepting black subservience. Different styles were developed and various denominations were observed... but there were a few similarities between these establishments that both catalyzed and hindered black progression.

The Good

The black church's sense of community is both a blessing and a curse. It's importance and authority has allowed it to be a frequent target of exploitation. But to address the bad and the ugly, we must talk about what makes the church so good. What makes it such a pillar of our community? Statistics show that black people are more likely to go to church than their peers. This is because the black church was, and continues to be, a safe haven. It shelters its flock from hunger, ignorance, white society, and the elements... and has been doing so for years. During reconstruction and Jim Crow, it was black churches doling out meals, administering educations, and organizing clothing drives. The church provided a sense of community and kinship that no other organization has. That is why it was a powerful hub of political and social activity during the fight for civil rights. It was where leaders and common folk gathered for news and strategizing. Without the black church, the civil rights movement wouldn't have happened. Lastly, on a more trivial level, many of our black music legends got 167 their start in black churches.

These are good things. Things that no black atheist, Muslim, Jew, or agnostic can deny. Unfortunately, the good does not obscure the bad, and it damned sure doesn't hide the ugly.

The Bad

When it was revealed that Wells Fargo sent black employees to black churches to push costly subprime loans, I wasn't surprised. When white politicians flex and pose in photo opps with black church leaders and later stay silent on relevant black issues post-election, again I'm not surprised. Because black ministers have historically had to fulfill the additional role of political leader, they were often subject to racial agendas that threaten to unravel what the church itself was trying to encourage-progression. Henry Ford, white American hero, donated to black churches and threatened to cut off support to those who didn't discourage labor unions among congregants. In the 1920s Ford employed about 1600 workers in Detroit, and they were assigned to the dirtiest and dangerous of jobs. Growing increasingly frustrated with immigrant employees looking to unionize, Henry Ford made sure to cozy up to various black church leaders throughout the 20s and 30s, on the lookout for "very high type fellows- those who were not black militants." Using the black church like a twisted job fair, Henry Ford sought to build a constituency of workers to be loyal to him. In the process of securing jobs for their congregants by being cool with Henry Ford, pastors became indebted to him politically.

This reminds me of black pastors who —knowingly or

unknowingly— aligned themselves with the enemy during the Bush administration. Prominent black pastors joined the predominately white Christian right to attack the LGBT community. Why? They "were on board and in hot pursuit of the federal faith-based funding that represented relief and an opportunity to expand their ministries." Reverend T.J. Graham of Nashville said he'd support Klansmen at his anti-gay rallies. Reverend James Meeks of Chicago is virulently anti-gay and is one of the leading voices in anti-gay marriage legislation in Illinois. But the biggest name of all was Bishop Eddie Long, of New Birth Baptist Church. For both aligning himself with the white Christian right and his degradation of black LGBT, he received one million dollars from the US Administration for Children and Families. Other ministers from T.D. Jakes to Willie Wilson have been noted for pushing homophobia onto their flocks, despite a central message of Christianity regarding loving thy neighbor. But, it's deeper than that.

The black pastor is expected to lead his flock selflessly. Unfortunately, the black pastor is revered and greatly respected, sometimes past the point of doubt or critique. Take the three most popular black preachers of the 20th century. Over his lifetime the pastor Sweet Daddy Grace owned 42 mansions, and he only wore the best of clothes and traveled in the nicest of cars. Meanwhile, his congregants, of the United House of Prayer, were largely poor southerners who faithfully tithed their 10% every Sunday. He advocated for one-man leadership, crowning himself as the sole trustee of the church's finances. He flipped the funds to fund his lavish lifestyle. In the present day, House of Prayer has 30-50,000 congregants. Sweet Daddy Grace's two contemporary rivals were similar swindlers.

Prophet Jones of Detroit was presented with lavish gifts and piles of money from his congregants every year for his birthday. The eight-day celebration was deemed a holiday and replaced Christmas. He was the same man who fancied himself "God's sole representative on Earth", even going as far to claim healing powers and psychic abilities. His followers were also a majority of poorly educated southern blacks, who had migrated to Detroit. To make matters worse, it wasn't his thievery that brought about his downfall. It was the revelation that he was a homosexual. Father Divine of New York, who preached zero tolerance abstinence, used land and property owned by his flock to keep up his lifestyle. He regularly took money from his followers, even once getting sued by one of them. He claimed to be divine, Jesus Christ reborn. Despite promoting anti-lynching legislation, Father Divine believed and preached that blacks perpetuate their own oppression by thinking racially.

Money has been a driving factor for many evangelical churches in this country, and not just the black ones... word to Jim Bakker. But it is not always money that brings out the bad in black churches. Here in the 21st century, scandals of prominent black preachers remind us how powerful these men are in the community— and how much they can get away with if they operate unchecked. Scandals like infidelity, tax evasion, embezzlement, and child abuse. Eddie Lee Long, the late senior pastor of New Birth Missionary Church, regularly denounced homosexuals, while also benefitting from Bush's faith-based initiative. So virulent was his homophobia that when four male former members risked public shame to accuse him of sexual abuse, his congregation barely blinked an eye. Long denied all accusations and settled out of court. This brings me to the ugly.

The Ugly

The black church is rigid with homophobia and hypocrisy. At my church, there was a trans woman that everybody claimed to be praying for but nobody actually talked to. She was one of the first transwomen I ever encountered, with three-inch acrylic talons elaborately painted and ruthlessly maintained. When the pastor opined against deviance, heads would slightly turn towards single mothers or the transsexual woman, if she happened to be in church that day. I remember hearing adults talk shit about her in the church parking lot, but it barely registered to me back then. She was just another. She was one of the people who stuck out, like girls rocking blue jeans instead of Sunday dresses.

"She should be ashamed of herself, dressing like she's running errands," one of my least favorite aunts would say over a cigarette, narrowing her eyes at some unfortunate victim who probably had nothing else to wear to service that morning. Even though the preacher would say "come as you are", my church was the kind of place where you came to impress. Who could wear the best outfit? Who was seen tipping the most cash in the collection plate? Who screamed amen the loudest? Who was willing to jump up from their seat and run, shoeless, up to the front of the church every Sunday, screaming thank you? It was all so theatric. It didn't seem real. And yet, so much of what the church influenced was very real. I've not only read the studies in academic journals that state many black churches condemn homosexuals, but I've been there to receive those messages myself. Those messages are why I sat up at night for hours as 171 a child, praying to God to make me straight and normal.

Studies have shown that among black men, "regular church attendance was significantly associated with more homophobic attitudes towards gay males." This stems from a long pattern of respectability politics, pushed by the black church in the face of American racism. As noted by Angelique Harris, "Post-slavery, to distance itself from [the] negative portrayal of black sexuality, the black community embraced a very conservative stance towards sex and deviant sexuality, such as pre-marital sex, extramarital affairs, out of wedlock births, and especially homosexuality." Respectability is a key aspect of the black church's existence and has unfortunately created a culture of intolerance for the community. Bayard Rustin, a key organizer of the civil rights movement and Martin Luther King's close friend, was shunned by the Southern Christian Leadership Conference when revelations about his sexuality were made. Untold numbers of Bayard Rustins were held back from their full potential to make others comfortable. This culture contributed to the social hierarchy that has given so much power to pastors, while also increasing homophobia and sexual double lives among church members.

Y'all know what I'm talking about. Sermons and whispers about faggots, sissies, deviants, and homos keep gay congregants in the closet, but they're the ones who often organize the dance recitals and dominate the choirs. In a 2010 study reaffirmed by findings in 1997, it was found that congregants often know about the sexual orientation of their "choir directors, lead singers, ushers, organists, deacons, and even pastors," but it is rarely discussed openly. But not talking about homosexuality in church (apart from quoting Leviticus) has led to a neglect of the AIDS crisis in the black community.

The initial 1981 report about H.I.V. listed five homosexual men to be infected, all rightfully assumed to be white. The report didn't mention the two black men- one a gay American and the other a straight Haitian- also infected with the virus. Like most of the country in the 1980s, the black community believed that AIDS was reserved for homosexuals. Even more specifically, most believed AIDS was for white homosexuals. While whispers about gay church members had already existed, the AIDS crisis intensified things. A number of young male members of black churches began to die from a mysterious 'cancer' in the mid-80s and early 90s. But it was the infection of basketball player Magic Johnson that sent a shockwave through the community. This forced some churches to acknowledge AIDS among black women (who were rapidly being affected), but in the present, many still don't like to talk about the virus, thanks to its stigma as the "gay disease". This is particularly true for more conservative southern denominations.

This is literally killing us. According to a recent article in *The New York Times*, "the Centers for Disease Control and Prevention ... predicted that if current rates continue, one in two African-American gay and bisexual men will be infected with the virus." H.I.V. rates are skyrocketing in southern states, where poverty, religiosity, lack of education, and stigma converge to leave people in the dark. Per the same article, "The South also has the highest numbers of people living with H.I.V. who don't know they have been infected, which means they are not engaged in lifesaving treatment and care — and are at risk of infecting others." This holds true despite the initiation of the Affordable Care Act, which increased the 173 number of people aware that they were living with H.I.V. The ACA played a big part in easing the HIV crisis that had worsened during the Bush Administration when little attention was paid to the virus in black-American communities. Instead, tax dollars were sent overseas to help nations in Africa. According to Greg Millett, senior policy adviser for the Obama administration's White House Office of National AIDS Policy, "The White House said H.I.V. is only a problem in sub-Saharan Africa, and that message filtered down to the public. Though the Bush administration did wonderful work in combating H.I.V. globally, the havoc that it wreaked on the domestic epidemic has been long-lasting."

Why does this matter to whoever is reading this? Two words: Donald Trump.

"The key to ending the AIDS epidemic requires people to have either therapeutic or preventive treatments, so repealing the A.C.A. means that any momentum we have is dead on arrival," said Phill Wilson, chief executive and president of the Black AIDS Institute in an interview with *The New York Times*. With the repeal of Obamacare looming over the country, black churches have a duty to increase AIDS awareness or we will be stepping back in time. HIV is not just for homosexuals, and the sooner black churches and their congregations detach the sin from the virus, the more lives will be saved. Early 21st century efforts to attack the AIDS crisis in the black community were largely successful for women, but not for gay and bisexual men. "Between 2005 and 2014, new H.I.V. diagnoses among African-American women plummeted 42 percent, though the number of new infections remains unconscionably high — 16 times as high as that of white women. During the same time period, the number of new H.I.V. cases among young African-American gay and bisexual men surged by 87 percent."

Every time I listen to someone harp on about HIV being a punishment from God or a conspiracy of the government to kill black people, I tremble from the weight of the excuses. No matter what you believe, black men and women have the highest rates of HIV among all races and help won't be coming from the government. As reported by the New York Times, "Despite the higher H.I.V. diagnosis and death rates in the Deep South, the region received $100 less in federal funding per person living with H.I.V. than the United States overall in 2015." It was also mentioned that America would need to invest 2.5 billion dollars to fully attack the AIDS crisis among black men a cruel number for a country in the middle of slashing budgets left and right. With all of the power black churches have, they must all step up.

Strung Out?

Karl Marx is often quoted as writing "religion is the opium of the masses", but this is a misquoted fragment that lacks context.

> *Religious suffering is, at one and the same time, the expression of real suffering and a protest against real suffering. Religion is the sigh of the oppressed creature, the heart of a heartless world, and the soul of soulless conditions. It is the opium of the people.*

Marx was saying that religion serves a practical function to those suffering in the world, but it also makes them docile and complicit in their suffering.

To me, Marx was right to compare drugs to religion. When times get tough, some people turn to alcohol, sex, or drugs. Others turn to Jesus. Like drugs, religion alleviates pain and can provide fond memories. In the black community, religion has been a pleasurable way to escape the hardships of racism and poverty. This pleasure manifested itself in the black church. The music, the food, the dancing, the celebrations. Also like drugs, religion isn't just for pleasure. It has a practical function. It brings people together for greater purposes and can give life meaning. The black church, a legacy of the black Christian religion, has served as a safe haven and community resource, whether you believe Jesus Christ to be your savior or not. Black culture is so infused with the black church that it is impossible to talk about one and not the other.

Though the church is not my safe haven, it is one to millions of my brothers and sisters. I used to be interested in challenging people's belief in the Christian God, calling it a white supremacist drug for the black masses, but I realized that the "drug" is quite necessary to our progression. If I (an atheist) can admit this, then surely believers can admit that Christianity —and by extension black churches—teeters on the line between useful medicine and dangerous poison. The pleasant effects can camouflage very real issues like homophobia, sexual abuse, and financial exploitation. The pleasant effects run a risk of making us complicit in our own suffering. Please don't be too high to see that.

How Black Twitter Revitalized Black Power

When I first joined Twitter in 2009, I didn't see the point. I, like pretty much everyone else who ventured onto the nubile social media platform from Facebook, thought 140 characters was restrictive and fascist. So I retreated back to Facebook for two years, surrounded comfortably by school acquaintances and friends of friends who regurgitated my own narrow view of the world. My interactions online were limited to people in my pocket of the South. There were no challenges to insults about skin color or retribution for non-black users casually saying n gga. There were no intellectual conversations, just nostalgic wall games and fight videos captured on antiquated flip camera phones.

During spring break of 2011, I began using Twitter regularly. I was exposed to the same shit from facebook but in 140 character increments. But there was something else, too. There was "Shea Butter Twitter." It was a facet of black twitter that I ogled from afar. All of my locals called them the wack, nappy, bitter, pro-black bitches-and that just wasn't my style. Or at least at that time, it wasn't. I wore my hair permed and pressed. It was short and brittle from chemical heat damage, lank and boring like many other black girls before the natural movement took hold. I believed in black on black crime and I called girls who dared to have more self-confidence than me "slutty". I played into respectability politics both as a woman and a black person, leaving a trail of ugliness that seems like a lifetime ago. I shudder thinking about all of the ignorance that lies on my twitter from 2011 to 2014. But I also feel pride about how I have grown. I wasn't the only one, either. Black twitter sparked a revitalization of black empowerment and enlightenment for a lot of us.

It was a gradual process. The complaints I had about racism had long been shoved into the back of my brain, abandoned for my desire to never be "that" black person. The troublemaker. The nuisance. The one roasted in films as pro-black and illogical, conscious to the point of no return. The one who was a vibe killer. The one who was angry and bitter. After all, racism was over, as my 10th-grade civics teacher informed me. So I swallowed microaggressions and discrimination with a smile on my face. That is, until black twitter. There my complaints about racism were affirmed. Patterns of discrimination were identified. I realized that I wasn't alone. Condescending white women and entitled white men were not unique to me in Charlotte, North Carolina.

Like a woman's body during effective foreplay, twitter discourse stimulated me into full-on arousal. Things that I used to scroll past on the timeline suddenly held my attention. I followed new accounts. Instead of automatically rejecting ideas that seemed absurd, I looked further into them. By this time I was in college, and taking advantage of Ohio State's resources for further enlightenment became crucial. I picked up new information and read new books. I stopped perming my hair and began taking the concept of police brutality seriously. In my classes where I had initially decided to not be a troublemaker, I began to not care about white feelings.

All the while, I watched the tragedies of Trayvon Martin, Mike Brown and Tamir Rice blaze across my timeline, ingesting each appalling twist and turn with my black twitter peers. We all watched in horror as media outlets, celebrities, and politicians justified police brutality and black discrimination. With each high profile case my mentality became more serious and my vision a little clearer. I didn't know it, but my life's purpose was revealing itself to me. Inside, I was changing. My views no longer lined up with things I came to believe in childhood. Celebrities I used to love became stale pieces of my past obsession with superficial fame and hunger for money. Certain kinds of jokes were no longer funny. I became less judgemental. Black love bubbled inside of me. Arguments on my timeline about skin color, higher education choice, and why white lovers were better than black ones sickened me.

Black Twitter was the catalyst of my metamorphosis from ignorant and self-hating to informed and pro-black. It's where I got unfiltered and FREE information. When the Black Panther Party formed a weekly newsletter, they did so because they knew controlling the narrative and chin checking mainstream media was crucial. On Twitter, that is what we do. We share information and critique. Whether people like it or not. Between thirst traps, fly out stories, and pictures of food, there are conversations happening that we can not get anywhere else. It hasn't always been so pro-black and intellectual on twitter, but the only ones complaining about how it is now are the brainwashed and the enemy.

You know who I'm talking about. There is a slew of black Twitter users who love to say that Twitter isn't real life. Half of them are users who have been causing timeline havoc since the days of twitter jail and #teamfollowback, 30somethings who tweet daily for hours on end but still claim the app isn't a real part of their lives. The others are transplants from facebook or recent high school graduates pushing pyramid schemes who capitalize every word of their tweets and seem to not know how to pluralize "feminist". "Twitter used to be so much fun," they whine, furious that they can't joke about rape or call dark skinned girls cockroaches. "Ya'll make everything too deep," they say, agitated because they're unable to indulge in any meaningful discourse outside of body counts and $200 dates. These are the folks who have been using the app entirely wrong. They usually have the same qualities- misogynistic, colorist, divisive, self-hating- and it's all because they still don't see twitter (and by extension, black twitter) as the real world. It's puzzling.

Real people get on twitter and tweet their real thoughts, both good and bad. People get jobs (and lose them) because of twitter. People have found love on twitter.

There are people who exist solely on money they earn on twitter. To think that Twitter is imaginary is to ignore the history of social gatherings. The Greeks had symposiums and the French had salons. Nearly every civilization had parties. People traded ideas, flirted, boasted, networked, had a little fun, and even got into passionate arguments (or physical fights). Social networks are the exact same thing- just in a virtual setting. Quite frankly that's even better.

There are so many ways black twitter is used to em-power the community, and not just by education. Black love and empathy have both been bolstered. We are addressing mental health issues like never before. The black identity has been expanded to include more than just cis-people, which creates lanes for activism. Black people are getting paid in new ways thanks to the app. It is a literal marketplace for entrepreneurs, freelancers, and a job fair for the unemployed. Black Twitter has also legitimized our complaints of discrimination and racism, by obsessively cataloging the myriad of visual proof of white foolishness. Wanna see that time a white celebrity tweeted and deleted something racist? We've got the screenshot. Wanna see a video of police brutality that never would have made it to the media without black twitter retweets? Check the timeline.

But, like the original black power movement, black twitter is susceptible to infiltration, megalomania, and exploitation. In recent months there have been reve-lations about white people creating handles for black twitter to cause arguments and chaos. Some members of black twitter with blue checks who claim to be pro-black are misogynistic, colorist, or homophobic. Even worse? They lambast any critique as hating. Their   181 refusal to understand both racial AND gender privilege creates endless feuds and distractions. Lastly, there are white companies who scope our timelines for marketing ideas that they can turn into millions, without giving us a single penny. These are things we must be constantly aware of. These are things we must address.

When I first began regularly using twitter I had no idea of the impact it would have on my life. It was just an app to shoot the shit on because more and more family members were invading Facebook, pestering me with friend requests. But it grew to be so much more than that. Black Twitter can sometimes be a party, where it's just jokes and memes. Other times it's a collective audience of studio albums or mixtapes, full of scathing roasts or unbridled praise. But all the time it is a hub of black ideas and activism that is slowly empowering someone to learn about their history and reality in a world spoiled by white supremacy.

Where would we all go if the app were to spontaneously shut down?

Black Women and Their Hair

I remember when I first saw Solange's big chop. At the time, I was so confused. I was one of the many people who called it ugly. I looked at her face without hair framing it and became repulsed. This was in 2009, the same year I was a freshman in high school. My own hair was often doobie wrapped or flat ironed to a crisp. My hair never grew past the nape of my neck and was often puffy at the roots from new growth. I jumped at every chance I got to get my hair slicked down under a wig cap and camouflaged by a glued quick weave. Whenever my hair was replaced with yaki hair, I felt beautiful. I didn't get my first taste of virgin bundles until 11th grade. So when I saw Solange, who had money and hairstylists, with short natural hair, it didn't make sense. As Solange's big chop grew into a beautiful crown, I stubbornly permed the hell out of my hair for the next few years and sat through hundreds of hours of sew-in applications. Seeing Chris Rock's *Good Hair* didn't even change my mind. I struck down any suggestion to "go natural" from multiple friends during my freshman year of college. It wasn't until sophomore year, after a perm gone wrong and a realization that unhealthy straight hair was uglier than healthy natural hair, that I made the big chop. I'll never forget the feeling. My head felt lighter. I felt lighter. Ever since then I have never seen a head of natural hair that I didn't like.

Before slavery, an African woman's hair meant various things depending on the region and culture she hailed from. Intricate styles were common. Maintaining hair was important and sacred because it was a non-verbal tool for communicating tribe affiliations, age, marital status, and more. African women were surrounded by resources for their hair, like Shea and palm oils. They had time to actually maintain it. To put it simply, an African woman's hair was an integral part of her identity. During slavery, hairstyles and maintenance changed because the identity of the black woman changed. For one thing, on some plantations, slave women were not allowed to wear anything but scarves. Some southern states made scarves a requirement for slave women to distinguish them from free black women. Headscarves were associated with low status and destitution. It was an ugly mark of inferiority.

But scarves weren't the only way that slave women were made to feel aesthetically inferior. Without access to proper hair care products of the day, many slave women resorted to using toxic substances like kerosene, butter, and animal fat on their fragile strands. You also have to remember they often didn't have the time required for maintenance like washing, detangling, conditioning, and twisting... especially if they worked from sun up to sundown. For many, hair maintenance meant frequent braids, scarves, and dry misshapen Afros. With broken ends, damaged edges, and a plethora of stress to compound any damage from toxic chemicals, black hair was considered unattractive. It was shamed by white society and brainwashed black folk. The good hair versus bad hair dynamic was intensified from the not-so-subtle battle between house slaves and field slaves. Straight and fine hair was a white characteristic, and because whiteness was idealized it was made the standard of beauty among black people as well.

After emancipation, kinks and braids were negatively associated with slavery. Kinky unkempt hair not only reminded black women of the terrors and abuses of bondage but also terrified disgusted white society. So, black innovators set to work to find a way for black women to avoid negative comparisons to white women and their long and fine tendrils. Some women mixed lye and potato for straightened hair with disastrous results. Annie Malone entered the scene in the 1890s, with a primitive version of a relaxer. She eventually went on to create a door to door hair care company that included a popular "hair grower". In 1909, Garrett A Morgan noticed the chemical he was using had inadvertently straightened curly wooden fibers. He used the chemical to create a relaxer, which he started selling to men before finding a strong consumer base in black women. He also sold a pretty popping hot comb.

By 1912, hot combs were growing in popularity among black women as a way to straighten hair. Madam CJ

Walker's hair products also flourished during this time. Most black women were desperate for not only straightened hair, but hair that grew. Going to the local beauty shop for hair maintenance gradually became a popular weekly to bi-weekly expense. Like black barbershops, black beauty salons flourished in our communities. From the 1920s to 1960s black women stayed on par with national styles of the day, for both assimilation and trend value. Many black social clubs required that black women be the right complexion and hair grade.

The 1920s saw the popularity of finger waves. The 1930s were filled with low maintenance roller curl looks, which could be explained by the Great Depression. It's important to note that roller curls were NOT anything like natural curls. The 1940s, the years of the war, saw a lot of up-dos, thanks to the styles of factory working women everywhere. Throughout this time black women also wore wigs to achieve mainstream hairstyles. But in 1951, Christina Jenkins obtained a patent for what would become the foundation of the sew in. Before her process, people used bobby pins to secure weave to their scalps. The process she created was a long one, and resulted in a bulkiness and stiffness that would get you clowned today- but it was an innovative style for mid-century black women.

Maintaining straight and mainstream hair was socially important to black women well into the late 60s, but the pro-black movement brought out a lot of never before seen afros. Influenced by the likes of Angela Davis, Kathleen Cleaver, and others, natural hair was more of a statement against the establishment than it was a lifestyle choice.

Kinky hair had scared and offended white America from the very beginning and that didn't suddenly change in the 70s. A black woman wearing her hair natural was a personal choice that could bring about a lot of criticism. During the pro-black movement and especially after it began to slow down, wearing an afro could run you the risk of appearing militant, troublesome, and unemployable. But it wasn't just an unappealing choice to white people. Even folks in the black community saw natural hair as unattractive and the mark of radicalism. It also didn't help that shrinkage encouraged those "bald-headed scalawag" jokes we all remember from our childhoods. Natural hair wouldn't truly catch on in the mainstream black community until the 21st century, after the Jherri Curls, feathered hair, and yaki quick weaves prominently ran amok from the late 70s to early 2000s. But making the choice to wear natural hair still isn't easy today. Natural hair is at risk of being called unprofessional in the workplace. Hairstyles largely worn by black Americans, like braids and dreadlocks, are banned by certain employers. Friends and family members ask you what happened to your old style after debuting your big chop instead of giving a reassuring compliment.

Throughout American history, the black woman's hair has been debated and demonized by every race and gender. Natural hair is ugly. Wearing flaming red weave is too much, but brown 14 inch Indian Wavy is just right (and better than a tight 4C afro). If you wear weave or straighten your hair, you're self-hating. If you dye your natural hair blonde or wear blonde weave you're REALLY self-hating. If you're bald, you're ugly. Braids are ghetto. Headscarves in public are ratchet.

ENOUGH.

I'm tired of it. At the end of the day, through all of the irrelevant opinions, a few facts have emerged:

1. Black women's hair choices have been influenced or limited by employment opportunities and status.

2. The choices we have historically made about our hair (and that some of us still make) are to blend into white society.

3. Natural hair has largely been vilified up until the 2000ss. It has gone from a political statement to a true lifestyle.

4. Whether rocking an afro or pulling up to the function in butt length aqua blue Malaysian curly, black women can wear ANY hairstyle and get away with it. Don't @ me. Matter of fact, don't @ any black woman with negativity about their hair (unless they're being malignant and a track is showing or their wig is too shiny, you've got every right to comment).

I love changing up my look with extensions. I crave trips to the beauty supply store to look at products for my own hair and to try on new wigs. I adore my afro- but I'll admit it took a long time for me to get to this place. It took me a long time to see beauty in my tight curls. But when acceptance came, it took over. There is nothing anybody can tell me about my beautiful crown. When I first saw Solange's big chop, it was unnerving. She wore it confidently, and that was the scary part. My whole life, natural hair that wasn't loosed mixed girl curls was ugly. "Natural hair isn't for everybody", girls and women everywhere said, patting the itchy roots of their Brazilian deep wave or running a comb through their long relaxed strands. Throughout American history, we were made to hate our natural hair and see it as inferior to white women- but there was Solange, holding her head high. Thanks, girl.

Are You Black or a woman?

Blacks are born black. Women are born women. Both groups had no choice in the matter. Both groups are oppressed and discriminated against for various reasons. I find it 50% hysterical and 50% pathetic when I hear a black man or black woman denounce feminism as unnecessary, annoying, or dumb- especially when they regularly talk about inequalities and injustices regarding their skin color. Why? Defined, feminism is the advocacy of women's rights on the grounds of political, social, and economic equality to men. Pro-blacks advocate for black rights on the ground of political, social, and economic equality to whites. If you believe black people (and all minorities in general) deserve to be equal to white people, you shouldn't have a problem digesting the idea that women want to be equal to men. Im not here to debate the merits of coining the fight for women's equality as womanism or feminism- I'm here to tell you that it's impossible to be pro-black and against the ideology of either term. Basically, the fight for equality does not stop at skin color. If you can wholeheartedly believe that you shouldn't be discriminated against, mistreated, or expected to act a certain way for respect, all because of a skin color you were born into and didn't choose- then how can you not understand a woman's desire for the same things? C'mon. Don't be foolish. Stop regurgitating white supremacist rhetoric in the form of sexism.

Here's a few common quotes I see as a reaction to feminism and feminist arguments, and my responses to them.

"WOMEN AND MEN ARE TOO DIFFERENT TO BE EQUAL."

There was a time when many people thought blacks and other minorities were so physically, mentally, and emotionally different from whites that it predisposed them to destitution, crime, and irrationality... justifying racist laws and attitudes towards them. This was called scientific racism. Experts in the 1800s truly believed that blacks were perfectly fitted to be slaves because of their "primitive psychological organization." They even took it a step further and declared that northern free blacks suffered from mental disorders more than southern slaves, claiming that slaves who escaped were suffering from a case of the crazies. Despite all of the claims throughout the years that perpetuated the fallacy that minorities were lesser creatures and should therefore be relegated to subservient positions, said minorities have demanded equality and a better quality of life. When 191 told that we were too simple-minded to survive without massa taking care of us, we proved otherwise when given the opportunity. When told our men were too violent and illogical to walk past white women without raping them, we proved otherwise. When told we were too lazy to become millionaires, we disproved this a thousand times over. This is no different from the plight of women. We have been told we're too emotional for leadership positions, too illogical to make decisions, or too delicate to endure hardship without the aid of a man. Clearly, women everywhere have proven this wrong when given the opportunity. The "difference" excuse, used to justify unfair treatment- is just that, an excuse.

"MEN ARE IN CHARGE. THAT'S HOW IT'S ALWAYS BEEN."

If sticking to "what it's always been" was a thing, black people would still be slaves. This argument is lazy and irrelevant.

"WOMEN HAVE THE RIGHT TO VOTE, THEY CAN WORK ANYWHERE, THEY'VE GOT TV CHANNELS... WHY CAN'T THEY JUST BE SATISFIED? MISOGYNY ISN'T A THING ANYMORE"

You know how a racist will accuse blacks of being ungrateful or choosy because they demand more? "They've got a black guy in the white house, a channel just for them, a whole month to themselves, and black twitter. Racism doesn't exist anymore." says racist number one. Black people don't think they should simply settle for a black president and BET. We want cops to stop getting away with murdering our own. We want more of our people represented in the media- and not just in a stereotypical manner. We want to be able to talk about our problems without being told we're being greedy. How is this any different from feminists? Feminists aren't educating, working, and bitching this hard for anything less than complete equality and the right to choose our behavior without worrying about qualifying for respect. We want to be paid the exact amount that men are paid for the same work. We want sexual predators of all genders to be held accountable for their actions. We want to be the ones in charge of our reproductive rights- not crusty old men who don't even have periods or babies in the first place. We want to be able to wear what we want to wear without being sexually assaulted for it and later told we looked like sluts. We want a wider variety of our gender represented in media- and not just the stereotypical or attractive ones. We want more content created by us, for us. We want to be able to talk about our problems without being told we're being whiny and insufferable. We deserve it.

"THE BIBLE SAYS WOMEN ARE SUPPOSED TO BOW DOWN TO MEN."

If you really feel the need to bring the bible into an intellectual conversation, lemme h t you with this whopper: the bible says a lot of shit. Among said shit, it tells servants and slaves to be obedient to masters. This was (and still is, according to some modern racists) a way to justify the enslavement of blacks. How can you put such stock into a book that perpetuated your ancestor's enslavement and re-enforced the pillars of racism that are still in place today?

"WOMEN WHO WEAR SKANKY CLOTHES ARE ASKING FOR IT."

Are black men dressed in anything other than a business suit and tie asking to be stopped and frisked? Asking to be bullied by a cop? Asking to be called a thug or 193 criminal or anything else derogatory? No? So are women asking to be called sluts or disrespected? Try to answer this question without sounding stupid.

"THESE HOES AIN'T GOT NO SELF-RESPECT... AND FEMINISTS WANT ME TO RESPECT THEM?!"

Racists took the looting and rioting in Ferguson, Missouri after Mike Brown's death to be black people, as a whole, disrespecting themselves. They took the behavior of few, and attributed it to our entire group. To them, the looting was a legitimate reason to blindly support cops accused of murder no matter what. "Look at those niggers acting like monkeys in the street," sneers white boy Chad, who set a couch on fire on his lawn last year when state lost the championship. "How can they expect cops to treat them like anything but trash?" Who is Chad to say that angry rioters should be shot dead? Who is Chad to say that the actions of the few should represent the many? Furthermore, who is he to determine whether or not blacks should be respected based on behavior that can be attributed to anybody?

It's no different than when someone sees a woman who is scantily clad, or dancing at a club, or generally enjoying her life. How is she a "hoe" because you got cheated on by a girl who wore the same type of clothing as her? How is she undeserving of respect because she talks about her sex life on twitter, when you talk about it too? How does she not respect herself because she likes to hit the club every weekend? Tons of men- whose sense of self-respect you never question- hit the club every weekend. Stop with this repugnant rhetoric. Your definition of self-respect is not applicable to others, and vice versa. People, including racists and misogynists, only use the self respect argument on people they never intended on respecting in the first place. You just want a valid reason to treat them as your inferior. This is how people have always done horrible things to other human beings- rationalizing the abuse or discrimination as something the victim deserved. Remember that many of the hundreds of thousands of women who are sexually and physically assaulted every year are considered to be undeserving of respect by someone.

"FEMINISM IS JUST CODE FOR MAN HATING"

Are you aware that there are white supremacists and "im not a racist but..." racists alike who claim that pro-black people are anti-white? If so, you're probably aware that there are indeed pro-black people who are anti-white. Does that mean that the minority who feel that way should be the reason the entire movement becomes de-legitimized? When those four black Chicago teens assaulted a white disabled man, racists were quick to link the event to Black Lives Matter to discredit the movement. Those teens did not speak for the ideology of Black Lives Matter, or the people who believe in it. When you say you don't believe in feminism because of the rogue misandrists, you're' not fooling me. You wouldn't believe in feminism even if there weren't any misandrists. Like white supremacists who ignore all the positives to zero in on the negatives, you are afraid of change and losing the privileges extended to you because of your gender.

Sidenote: Women who say that feminism is code for man-hating are just afraid to look like man-haters for the sake of their dating lives. Women who balk at feminism with incredulity are looked at with the same mixture of pity and annoyance as black uncle toms. In brevity, you're brainwashed. I hope one day you wake up. Don't @ me.

"FEMINISTS WANT TO EMASCULATE BLACK MEN AND RUIN THE BLACK FAMILY"

It's a little telling that to some men, women's equality means their doom. Its frighteningly similar to white people who claim that pro-black people want to strip white people of their power and ruin America. This irrationality is a manifestation of guilt and fear that the oppressed will treat their oppressors with the same cruelty and discrimination that they have experienced. You're scared that women gaining rights means that your power will be reduced. Like white people afraid to lose the privileges they enjoy, as a black man you are reluctant to lose the privileges you have. Furthermore, because part of your identity as a black man ranges from feeling compelled to lead black women to believing yourself to be completely superior to them, feminism threatens your masculinity. Deep down you're thinking how can you be I truly be a black man if black women are my equals? You've got to shred this way of thinking.

FEMINISM IS FOR WHITE WOMEN

You think you have a point, but you don't. Feminism has had a long history of excluding or using women of color, but for quite a while now, intersectional feminists and feminists focused on black women (some call themselves black feminists, others simply say 'womanists') have done their part to fill in gaps that some selfish white feminists left behind. Early black feminist activities include 19th century clubs like the National Association of Colored Women and activism by figures like Ida B. Wells and Mary Church Terell. Not all black feminists always insert the "black" when identifying with feminism, but you better believe that's what they are.

Feminism is not a perfect ideology, but its core meaning remains unchanged. Either you agree with it or you don't. But if you don't believe in it, don't be silly enough to also claim to be pro-black.

I did not choose to be born black or a woman. I did not ask to be rejected by racist white women or misogynistic black men. I did not ask to be restrained by racism or sexism, therefore I fight against both. If you ever ask me to abandon either battle in favor of the other, my verbal rebuke will probably cause you to call me an angry black bitch.

ABOUT THE AUTHOR

Elexus Jionde, AKA Lexual, was born January 26th, 1994. She is a graduate of The Ohio State University with a B.A. in History. She creates and curates content for Intelexual Media, a digital learning and entertainment platform with an emphasis on history and black culture. In addition to a passion for learning new things she has unhealthy obsessions with iced coffee and pictures of pit bull puppies. You can visit Intelexual Media at intelexual.co

Made in the USA
Middletown, DE
10 September 2020